HMS AMBUSCADE

From 1746 to the Present Day

By
Dave Watson

HMS Ambuscade
From 1746 to the Present Day

Copyright © Dave Watson 2024
ISBN: 978-1-80443-074-3

The right of Dave Watson to be identified as the author of this book has been asserted by him in accordance with the Copyright, Designs and Patents Act of 1988.

All rights reserved. No part of this book may be reproduced or transmitted in any form or by any means, electronic or mechanical, including photocopying, recording or by any information storage and retrieval system, without the prior permission of the author in writing.

Every reasonable effort has been made to trace copyright holders and to obtain their permission for the use of copyright material. The author and publisher apologise for any errors or omissions in this work, and would be grateful if notified of any corrections that should be incorporated in future reprints or editions of this book.

F172 cover photo Leo Marriott/Air Sea Media

Published by:
Balkan Military History
www.balkanhistory.org

CONTENTS

INTRODUCTION 4

CHAPTER ONE: THE FIRST HMS *AMBUSCADE* 7

CHAPTER TWO: THE FIRST BRITISH-BUILT HMS *AMBUSCADE* . . 20

CHAPTER THREE: THE FIRST WORLD WAR 45

CHAPTER FOUR: THE SECOND WORLD WAR 64

CHAPTER FIVE: TODAY'S HMS *AMBUSCADE* 78

CHAPTER SIX: CONCLUSION 104

APPENDIX 1 - CAPTAINS OF HMS *AMBUSCADE* 106

APPENDIX 2: SHIPBUILDING ON THE RIVER CLYDE 110

FURTHER READING 113

ACKNOWLEDGMENTS 116

ABOUT THE AUTHOR 117

INTRODUCTION

HMS Ambuscade is the name given to a number of Royal Navy ships between 1746 and 1993. The final ship of that name (a Type 21 frigate) was sold to Pakistan in 1993 and renamed PNS Tariq. In 2023, the Pakistan Navy (Pākistān Bahrí'a) kindly agreed to donate the ship to the charity Clyde Naval Heritage. The charity plans to bring the ship back to the Clyde, where it was built, as a museum, with a focus on the Falklands War due to its service in that conflict. That plan inspires this book, and all the profits from the book will be donated to the Clyde Naval Heritage.

The aim of this book is to describe the ships named Ambuscade and their operational history. There were five substantive ships of that name, although matters were more complex during the Napoleonic Wars when one Dutch and two French warships were renamed Ambuscade after being captured by the Royal Navy. The Royal Navy's first steam-powered frigate was laid down in 1830 and was initially named Ambuscade. However, it was renamed HMS Amphion when launched in 1846.

While not a Royal Navy ship, there was an earlier British fighting ship named Ambuscade. She was a privateer, authorised by the British government to attack enemy ships during the War of the Spanish Succession (1701-1714). She was armed with 30 guns and had a crew of 140. This was a profitable business, as can be seen from the court records, for both the owners (Portsmouth and London merchants) and the government. For example, in 1711, Ambuscade captured the French ship Excellent (master Stephen Raffin), laden on the banks of Newfoundland with 4,300 fish, bound for a port in France.[1]

---

[1] TNA, Captured ships, HCA 32/57

The word *ambuscade* is typically defined as 'an ambush' (noun) or 'to ambush or lie in ambush' (verb). The English language adopted *ambuscade* in the late 16th century, borrowing it from Middle French, whose speakers had raided Old Italian to acquire it. The French had made *embuscade* from *imboscata*, which was from *imboscare*, 'to place in ambush.' Evidence of *ambush* functioning as a verb can be found as far back as the dawn of the fourteenth century. It arrived not from Middle French (French as spoken in the fourteenth to sixteenth centuries) but from Anglo-French, the French spoken in medieval England. Its second syllable is from the Old French *busc*, meaning 'forest, grove.' The first known use of *ambuscade* was in 1588.[2]

It was the French Navy that first named its ships *Embuscade*, and the name entered the Royal Navy through the capture of a French frigate in 1745. Throughout its history in the Royal Navy, the name has been given to frigates or destroyers, whose design and role included ambushing enemy ships. The frigate in the age of sail was the Royal Navy's glamour ship, big enough to carry significant firepower but fast enough to evade larger enemies. They were the light cavalry of the seas, patrolling, scouting and above all, fighting. As Admiral Nelson said, they were 'the eyes of the fleet'. They often fought ship-to-ship actions, which made frigate captains famous through contemporary press coverage and even today through the fictional stories of Hornblower and others. They often operated alone, while the larger ships of the line typically operated in squadrons or fleets to blockade enemy ports.

An introductory word on language. Royal Navy ships are given the prefix HMS (Her or His Majesty's Ship), while the French Navy does not use prefixes for its ships. Naval guns were typically described by the weight in pounds of the solid projectile (cannon balls in the age of sail)

---

[2]Merriam-Webster's Dictionary (11th edition, 2003)

fired from the ship's guns; hence, 'pdr' (pounder) is used in the text. The number of guns on a ship is often put in brackets after the name, e.g. HMS *Ambuscade* (40). Ship dimensions usually include its overall length, the length of the keel (base of the ship), and the beam (width).

Royal Navy ranks will be referenced throughout the book. In the age of sail, HMS *Ambuscade* was commanded by an officer with the rank of Captain. In the Royal Navy, any officer in command of a ship was accorded the honorific 'Captain', but only a post-captain could command a ship of one of the six major rates like *Ambuscade*. This was the highest rank in the Royal Navy below that of rear-admiral, except that for detached duty, a captain could be temporarily given the rank of commodore and would then rank above all other captains in the squadron. After rear-admiral, an officer could be promoted to vice-admiral. A full admiral usually commanded one of the three squadrons into which a British fleet was divided. The squadrons were distinguished by colour, with the order of precedence being red, white, and blue; the admirals commanding the squadrons flew corresponding coloured ensigns. All levels of admiral are described as flag ranks.

BATTLE HONOURS

FINISTERRE 1747 - LAGOS 1759 - JUTLAND 1916 - ATLANTIC 1940-44 - ARCTIC 1942 - FALKLANDS 1982.

CHAPTER ONE:
THE FIRST HMS *AMBUSCADE*

The first HMS *Ambuscade* was built at Le Havre, a major port on the estuary of the river Seine in the Normandy region of northern France. The ship was a one-off design by Pierre Chaillé, launched as *L'Embuscade* on 19 March 1745 as a frigate for the French Navy. The frigate was 132 feet, 6 inches (40.4m) long overall, with a keel of 107 feet, 5.5 inches (32.8m) and a beam of 36 feet (11m). In keeping with French practice, this was a large frigate with twenty-six 8-pdrs and twelve 4-pdrs. A frigate of this period was built with an unarmed lower deck, which meant it could heel considerably and carry sail even in strong winds. It could maintain higher speeds in lighter winds and keep its gun ports open longer than larger ships.

Ambuscade at the River Plate in 1763 (from a painting by William Elliot in the UK Government Art Collection)

However useful though frigates were, the strength of a navy was measured in ships of the line. This designation related to three-masted ships with between sixty and one hundred guns. Frigates could not get near enough to engage their bigger guns. Advances in sail handling meant that eighteenth-century ships could keep their sails full even within seventy degrees of the wind, although captains sailed with the wind behind them whenever possible. The worst fate was to become becalmed.

In 1746, Britain and France were at war as part of the broader War of the Austrian Succession (1740-1748). The war was about maintaining the balance of power in Europe, although the pretext was the right of Maria Theresa to succeed her father, Emperor Charles VI, as ruler of the Habsburg monarchy. The Habsburgs were based in Austria, but in this period, the empire included parts of the Balkans, Austrian Netherlands, Hungary and other parts of central Europe. France, Prussia, and Bavaria saw the war as an opportunity to challenge Habsburg power, while Britain, the Dutch Republic, and Hanover backed Maria Theresa. As the conflict widened, it drew in other states, including Spain, Sardinia, Saxony, Sweden, and Russia. Britain and France also competed for global colonies, particularly in India, where they fought a series of conflicts known as the Carnatic Wars.

While there were few major sea battles during this conflict, control of the seas was vital for a nation like Britain that relied heavily on commerce. The Royal Navy's task was to secure British trade, stifle the enemy's trade, move troops by sea, destroy the enemy fleet and attack enemy coasts. Merchant ships were encouraged to sail in convoys escorted by warships, but many went ahead alone to secure commercial advantage. The British maritime tradition infused naval commanders with boldness, supported by experienced crews and the financial resources to maintain fleets at sea for long periods. Tactics were relatively simple, as there were limited opportunities to manoeuvre at sea. An admiral would hope for a numerical advantage and lay his superior firepower alongside the enemy fleet in a formation called line of battle ahead. Cannon fire might shatter the hull of the enemy ship, but damage to the rigging was more common, and dismasting would quickly immobilise a ship, allowing it to be captured. Captains and crew shared prize money, which related to the value of the ship and, in the case of merchantmen, its cargo.

Britain in 1746 was the dominant naval power, if not as strong as it would become later in the century. The French Navy, while strong on paper, was suffering from years of neglect brought about by a shortage of funds. In 1744, a 25-strong French fleet commanded by Admiral Comte de Roquefeuil declined to face a similar-sized British fleet under Admiral John Norris at The Downs (off the Kent coast). This action ensured that the French could not adequately support Bonnie Prince Charlie and the Jacobite rising of 1745. The Dutch Republic added their fleet to the British strength, although little was achieved in northern waters during the War of the Austrian Succession.

On 24 March 1746, *L'Embuscade* was attacked by HMS *Defiance*, a 58-gun fourth-rate ship of the line in the English Channel. In an unequal struggle, the French ship was captured and taken to Plymouth. She was renamed *Ambuscade* on 28 May 1746 after being refitted and up-gunned with twenty-six 12-pdrs and fourteen 6-pdrs. The design worked so well for the Royal Navy that it set a precedent for the Royal Navy's 32-gun and 36-gun frigates of the 1750s.[3] It was accepted that French naval technology was superior, leading the British to copy their designs.

Ambuscade had a crew of 250 commanded by Captain Lucius O'Brien. He was commissioned as a lieutenant in 1737 and served in the Russian Navy in 1739, which was not an uncommon career path then. He returned to serve in the Royal Navy in March 1744, commanding HMS *Portsmouth* (24) with the rank of commander. In December 1745, he was promoted to captain of HMS *Sheerness* (24). His ship played a role in defeating

---

[3] R.Winfield, British Warships of the Age of Sail, 1714-1792, (Seaforth, 2007).

the Jacobite uprising by capturing the sloop *Le Prince Charles* (14) (the renamed *Le Hasard*) off the coast of Scotland near the Kyle of Tongue on 25 March 1746. The French ship carried £13,000 in gold, weapons and supplies for the Jacobites. The money was subsequently taken by government troops on land from Lord Loudon's Regiment and loyalist clansmen in an action known as the Skirmish of Tongue. This severe blow to the Jacobite cause contributed to the final defeat at the Battle of Culloden.

The report in the *London Gazette* said:

'Captain O'Brian of Sheerness man of war, now off this place giving an account that after chasing the *Le Prince Charles* above 56 leagues he drove her ashore and obliged the French and Spaniards who were in her to quit her and to land, which they did with five chests of money to the value of £12,000 and upwards.'[4]

After three months commanding *Ambuscade*, O'Brien was promoted to command HMS *Colchester* (50), subsequently fighting in several naval actions before reaching the rank of Rear Admiral of the White in October 1770.

Captain John Montagu took command of the frigate in January 1747. Ambuscade was part of Admiral George Anson's fleet at the First Battle of Cape Finisterre on 14 May 1747. Fourteen Royal Navy ships of the line, with Ambuscade as the sole frigate, attacked a French convoy of thirty ships with supplies for the French colonies in North America (modern Canada), commanded by Admiral de la Jonquière. The escorting French warships were heavily outnumbered, but fought for five hours until seven in the evening. The British captured four ships of the line, two frigates, and seven merchantmen, with over £300,000 in coins (nearly

---

[4]London Gazette (15 April 1746)

John Montagu (1719-1795)

£60 million at today's prices) on board. *Ambuscade* captured the French merchant ship *La Thétis* of Nantes with letter of marque (730 tons, 20 guns, 95 men). It was carrying gunpowder, brandy, wine, sailcloth, beef and flour.[5]

John Montagu went on to command ships of the line, was the MP for Huntingdon, governor of Newfoundland, and ended his naval career as Admiral of the White. He was regarded as being of great integrity and benevolent but could also be intemperate, foul-mouthed and base, prone to complaining somewhat irreverently about his wife's bulk!

The War of the Austrian Succession ended with the Treaty of Aix-la-Chapelle in 1748, which allowed time for *Ambuscade* to be repaired and then refitted before returning to service, commanded by Captain Joshua Rowley. The ship's log for this period describes patrols and anti-smuggling actions in the Channel.[6] War broke out again in Europe and the colonies in 1756. This was the Seven Years' War (1756-1763), often called the first world war, reflecting the global nature of the conflict. Britain was allied with Prussia and others on the continent against France, Spain and Austria. The naval war was fought in the English Channel with raids on the French coast, and in support of attacks on French colonies in the West Indies, North America and India.

At the outbreak of war, *Ambuscade* was serving with the fleet in The Downs before being sent to the Mediterranean in October 1756 under

---

[5]TNA, Captured ship: La Thétis of Nantes (master François Masson), HCA 32:155
[6]TNA, Ambuscade Ship's Log, ADM 51/35

the command of Captain Richard Gwyn until August 1759. The naval war in the Mediterranean was not going well for the British, with the defeat at the Battle of Minorca on 20 May 1756 forcing the navy back to Gibraltar. The loss of Minorca led to the controversial court-martial and execution of the British commander, Admiral John Byng, for 'failure to do his utmost' to relieve the siege. As Voltaire put it, 'In this country, it is thought wise to kill an admiral from time to time to encourage the others.' While serving in the Mediterranean, *Ambuscade* captured the French privateer *Le Vainqueur* (24) on 12 July 1757. Almost a year later, together with HMS *Lyme*, they destroyed *La Rose* (24). The ship's muster book for June to August 1759 reports a complement of 250 seamen, 39 marines and 35 supernumeraries, with fairly low sickness levels.

The Royal Navy's position in the Mediterranean was recovered at the Battle of Lagos (off southern Portugal) on 18-19 August 1759, when Sir Edward Boscawen's fleet destroyed an outnumbered French fleet under Jean-François de La Clue-Sabran. The French fleet in two divisions sailed past Gibraltar, unaware that the British fleet was disorganised due to repairs. Boscawen got his fleet organised and gave chase in what was described as 'a splendid feat of seamanship...such as only seamen who know the Rock can fully appreciate.'[7] Due to confused orders, the two French divisions split, and la Clue may have thought the pursuing British were his missing division. The French also lost the wind, and the British caught them. Outnumbered, *Centaure* (74) was captured, and others started to suffer severe damage, so la Clue signalled a retreat.

Two French ships of the line were destroyed, and a further two were captured when pinned in Portuguese waters. The remainder were blockaded in Cadiz. La Clue was mortally wounded. *Ambuscade* was listed as present at the battle (although the ship's log does not record any action), but frigates generally did not engage larger ships in actions of this kind. Their role was to pass intelligence, shadow the enemy and repeat signals to ships out of sight of the flagship. The fighting was left to the heavily gunned ships of the line.

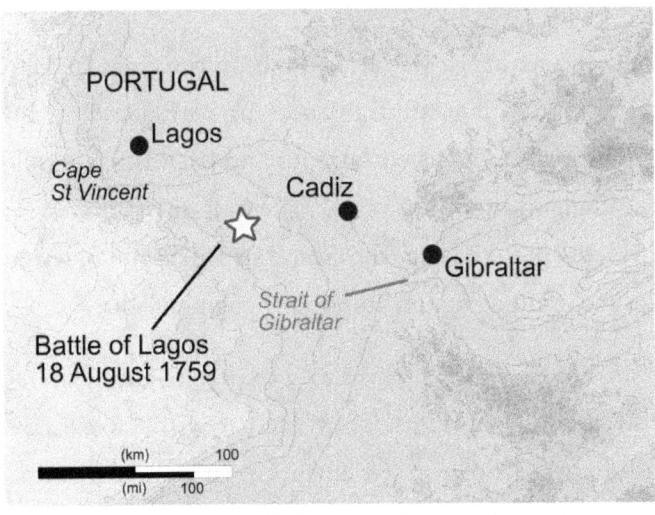

Amitchell125, CC BY-SA 4.0

---

[7] N. Tracy, The Battle of Quiberon Bay 1759 (Pen & Sword, 2010), Loc.2156.

The last commander of *Ambuscade* was Captain Christopher Basset. He had entered the navy from the merchant service and was a Cornish protégée of Admiral Boscawen. He was present at the Battle of Lagos, commanding HMS *Rainbow* (44). He transferred to *Ambuscade* after the battle, swapping ships with Captain Gwyn.

The French invasion threat to the British Isles ended at the Battle of Quiberon Bay (off the French coast near Saint-Nazaire) on 20 November 1759, when Sir Edward Hawke's fleet defeated the French fleet commanded by Marshal de Conflans.

The war ended in 1763 with Britain ending French power in India and throwing the French out of Canada. However, *Ambuscade* had been surveyed for damage and paid off in May 1761. A severe gale off the Scillies, lasting four days, was encountered while returning *Ambuscade* from Gibraltar in 1760. Captain Bassett reported that it 'occasioned the ship to spring a leak that has obliged me to pump her every half hour since.' This was probably not caused by her construction; four days of gales would have strained any ship.

The lengthy service at sea was also tough on the crew. In March 1761, the captain wrote to the Admiralty seeking permission for his crew to be allowed ashore to visit their families and friends, saying, 'They have been from England about five years.'[8] The welfare of his crew was clearly of concern to Captain Basset. The Admiralty file is full of letters seeking discharges for injured seamen and bonus payments due.

In February 1762, *Ambuscade* was sold to private adventurers for £805 (£136,000 at today's prices). They used it with *Lord Clive* (60) to unsuccessfully attack Spanish settlements in La Plata (Argentina) early in 1763 under the overall command of Captain John Macnamara. This was

---

[8]TNA, Captain Basset letters, (March 1761), ADM 1:1492.

an attack on a Spanish colony with the intent to invade and pillage when Britain was not at war with Spain. In these circumstances, the letters of marque issued to privateers did not apply, and the officers captured by the Spanish were hanged.

A privateer was a ship that engaged in maritime warfare under a commission, also referred to as a letter of marque, during wartime. A government issued the commission and empowered the holder to carry on all forms of hostility permissible at sea by the usages of war. This included attacking foreign vessels and taking them as prizes. The proceeds from captured ships were divided by percentage among the privateer's sponsors, ship owners, captains and crew. A percentage share usually went to the issuer of the commission (i.e. the sovereign). Privateering allowed countries to raise revenue for war by mobilising privately-owned armed ships and sailors to subsidise state power. For participants, privateering provided the potential for a greater income and profit than was obtainable as a merchant seafarer.

It was regular practice in this period for the navy to be run down after a war, with ships sold off or mothballed. Officers were typically put on half-pay, with a much smaller navy retained to defend the colonies against piracy or rebellion.

Serving in the Eighteenth-Century Navy

Life in the Royal Navy during the eighteenth century could be brutal and short. Officers typically came from naval families, even dynasties, and the navy provided a socially acceptable profession for younger sons without financial resources. If you survived, it could also be lucrative thanks to prize money, particularly on a frigate like *Ambuscade* at an appropriate station at a time of war. Being a successful naval officer and reaching flag rank depended on being born at the right time to take advantage of the outbreak of war. You also needed family or other 'interest', a sponsor to take you under their wing to help you get a good naval posting. Once appointed, professional expertise was vital, along with good health. Successful frigate captains demonstrated courage and seamanship; those without aptitude left the service.

A study of thirty-six naval officers by Anne McLeod concluded they 'had firstly to use the family or professional "interest" which got them into the navy; secondly, they had to make use of the stations to which they were sent to achieve fame and fortune; thirdly, they had to live long enough, and still be active, to be rewarded at the time of the next round of promotions.'[9] Recruitment of seamen at the time of war was always a problem for the Royal Navy. Volunteers could be found, particularly during periods of economic hardship, encouraged by bounties and legislation that laid down regular payments. Merchant seamen were an important source of recruits in wartime, and significant numbers were foreign citizens. Magistrates would also offer sea duty to criminals or local reprobates, who would otherwise burden the parish, although many of these were rejected as unfit for service. Impressment was resorted to in extremis, with the press gang entering public houses, lodging houses and other possible hiding places, searching for men. Preferably those with sea experience, who could be identified by their weather-beaten faces and rolling gait. Nevertheless, impressment was not popular in ports. In 1756, the mayor of Liverpool threatened to imprison any officer who pressed a man in his city, and the regulating captain was nearly killed in the ensuing riot.

---

[9] A. McLeod, The Mid-Eighteenth Century Navy from the Perspective of Captain Thomas Burnett and His Peers, (University of Exeter, 2010).

Respected captains could have 'followings', seamen who wanted, although not always allowed, to follow them from ship to ship. While discipline, including the lash, was harsh, captains understood that seamen were an expensive resource to be looked after. The level of flogging varied considerably from ship to ship. Ships' rations could be double that received by men serving on land, although the quality deteriorated quickly at sea, and scurvy or other diseases resulted. Rheumatism and consumption were the most common causes of discharge. Desertion was common, and leave was not regularly granted. In 1761, Captain Christopher Bassett was petitioned by the crew of *Ambuscade,* who wanted to go on leave after five years of service in the Mediterranean. He was permitted to give a month's leave 'to those who may be trusted among the crew'. Death from an accident or disease was more likely than from enemy action.

Cost-cutting almost certainly damaged the effectiveness of the Royal Navy in this period. For example, captains complained about the 'noxious air in ships', and Vice-Admiral Boscawen's fleet in 1755 lost some two thousand men to pernicious disease.[10] It wasn't until the Seven Years' War that the Admiralty copied other navies and installed ventilators on larger ships. Admiral George Anson was responsible for a wide range of reforms in the period 1751-1762, which prepared the Royal Navy for the challenges to come.

Another challenge for sailors in this period was navigation. They relied on dead reckoning, making their course where possible along the latitude of a prominent high cape such as Cape St Vincent. Even the captain of a crack warship lacked the capacity to plot his longitude. The 'lunar distance method' for calculating longitude was only discovered in the mid-eighteenth century. It required a sextant, clear sky, and a long and

---

[10] J.Krulder, Naval Dysfunctions at the Beginning of the Seven Years' War, (from Sailors, Ships and Sea Fights, Helion, 2024), p.237.

complicated calculation. John Harrison invented a chronometer that could plot a position in cloudy weather, which enabled Captain Cook's first round-the-world voyage in 1771. However, by 1802, only seven per cent of British warships had a chronometer on board. East India Company ships had at least one by 1810, but it didn't become standard Royal Navy issue in home waters until 1840. A Royal Navy captain complained in *The Naval Chronicle* of 1812, 'Every man who has associated with naval officers for the last thirty years, must have heard their complaints of the want of good chronometers, which few can afford to purchase, as they cost hundreds of pounds each.'[11]

For all the challenges facing seamen in the eighteenth-century Royal Navy, naval service could have its financial rewards. Captured enemy ships brought prize money, which was distributed according to rank. The admiral took his share with the captain in the first distribution, followed by the officers in the second and third distributions, and then the seamen in the fourth and fifth distributions. In the example below,[12] *Ambuscade* under Captain Richard Gwyn captured two French ships during his first command of the ship in June 1747. He received £406 (£74,500 at today's prices) for both ships. Senior officers got £60 (£11,000 today), and able seamen got less than £2 (£367 today). The admiral also got a cut worth £243 (£44,600 today). That's not bad, considering the admiral wasn't even present. The cash wasn't paid immediately; in this case, it was two and a half years later.

---

[11] R.Knight, Convoys, (Yale University Press, 2023), p.4.
[12] TNA, HCA 30:663.

We whose Names are underwritten on this & the following Pages contained in this Book, being the Officers & Company of His Majesty's Ship Ambuscade or the legal Representatives of such, as were actually on board, at the destroying two French Ships of War called the Etoile & Chameau on the 22 June & 5th July 1747, do acknowledge to have received at the times undermentioned of Thos Bell & Robt Weldon Agents for the said Officers & Ships Company the several Sums against our Names exprest, being in full of Our respective Shares of the Nett Proceeds of Bounty Bills made out to them in Our behalf for the said Service.

When Paid	Mens Names	Quality	For the Etoile	For the Chameau	Receipts	Witnesses
	First Distribution					
1749 Novr 18	Rt Honble Sir Petr Warren	Admiral	142 5 3	101 3 3	Paid pr Receipt	
1749 Decr 5	Richd Gwyn	Captain	284 10 6	202 6 6	John Bardd[illegible] attd to Capn	
	Second Distribution					
1749 Novr 20	Joseph Gage	1st Lieut	35 11 3¾	25 5 9¾	Henry Minchge — attd	
1749 Novr 18	John Carter Allen	2d do	35 11 3¾	25 5 9¾	Jno. Carter Allen	O Baxley
Decr 29	Henry Phillips	3d do	35 11 3¾	25 5 9¾	Paid pr Receipt	
1749 Novr 20	Joseph Marriott	Mar	35 11 3¾	25 5 9¾	Joseph Marriott	
	Third Distribution					
1749 Novr 20	John Blanchard	Gunr	14 4 6¼	10 2 3¾	Ed F Bridges for Wife Eliz. Attd	
Do	Richd Collins	Carpr	14 4 6¼	10 2 3¾	Ed F Bridges for Alexr Nasmith Attd	
Decr 5	Michl Willson	Acting Boatsn	14 4 6¼	10 2 3¾	Micl Willson	
1749 Decr 8	John Henderson	Surgn	14 4 6¼	10 2 3¾	Chas Hay Attye	
1749 [illegible] 9	Thos Winchelsea	Pursr	14 4 6¼	10 2 3¾	Edward Reed Attorney	
[illegible] 2	Patk Milne	Mas Mte	14 4 6¼	10 2 3¾	Patk Milne —	

CHAPTER TWO:
THE FIRST BRITISH-BUILT HMS *AMBUSCADE*

The first British-built HMS *Ambuscade* was a 32-gun fifth-rate frigate of the *Amazon* class, launched in Deptford on 17 September 1773. She was built by the firm of Adams and Barnard for a total cost of £11,346 (£1.4 million at today's prices). The overall length was 126 feet, 3 inches (38.48m), with a keel of 104 feet, 1 inch (10.71m). The beam was 35 feet, 1.75 inches (10.71m). She was armed with twenty-six 12-pdrs, six 6-pdrs, and six 18-pdr carronades. A carronade was a short, smoothbore cannon first produced by the Carron Company in Falkirk. Its primary function was to serve as a powerful, short-range, anti-ship and anti-crew weapon. The Royal Navy was initially reluctant to adopt this type of gun, and they didn't count in numbering the guns on a ship. Hence, *Ambuscade* was a 32-gun frigate that carried 38 guns, including carronades. However, they proved their effectiveness in battle, and other navies soon followed suit.

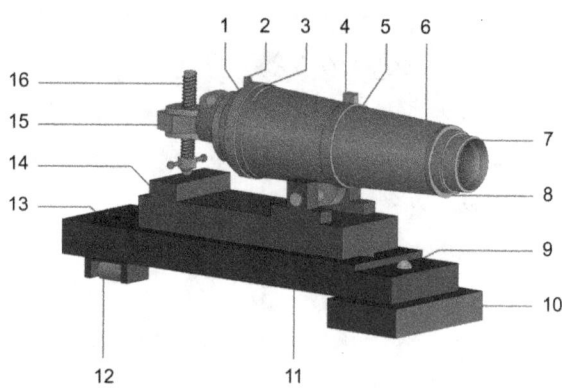

1. Breech bolt 2. Aft sight 3. Vent hole 4. Dispart sight 5. First reinforcing ring 6. Barrel 7. Muzzle 8. Second reinforcing ring 9. Azimuthal pivot 10. Chock 11. Elevation pivot 12. Wheel 13. Mobile pedestal 14. Carriage 15. Pommel 16. Elevation thread. (Delaby Pierre (Walké), CC BY-SA 3.0).

The ship was commissioned under Captain John Macartney at Chatham in January 1776 and sailed for North America in July 1776. *Ambuscade's* first captain had been commissioned as a lieutenant on 20 January 1756. He had served in North America during the Seven Years' War and returned there in 1774 in command of HMS *Mercury* (20). He was about to be court-martialled for allegedly engaging in a string of letters with a local mayor in Virginia, in which he had expressed his pain and reluctance at having to threaten the use of coercive force against any rebellious subjects. The charges were dropped, and he returned home to command *Ambuscade*.

The American Revolutionary War

The American Revolutionary War (19 April 1775 – 3 September 1783), also known as the American War of Independence, involved American Patriot forces under George Washington fighting against British and American Loyalists. The American Patriot forces were later supported by France (1778) and Spain (1779). The conflict was fought in North America, the Caribbean, and the Atlantic. The war secured the independence of the United States of America.

The United States Congress established the Continental Navy on 13 October 1775. For most of the war, the Continental Navy included a handful of frigates and sloops supported by 1,700 privateers. These privateers captured 2,283 enemy ships, seriously damaging the British war effort and global commerce. Most famously, in 1778, Captain John Paul Jones, born in Scotland, attacked British shipping in the Irish Sea in the USS *Ranger* and raided Whitehaven and St Mary's Isle near his birthplace of Kirkcudbright. The following year, he returned with a five-ship squadron, attacking merchant ships around the British Isles a d causing panic in Edinburgh before being halted at the Battle of Flamborough Head.

France sent Vice-Admiral Comte Charles Henri Hector d'Estaing with a fleet of twelve ships of the line to assist the Americans in April 1778. Bad weather kept the rival fleets apart, limiting combat to a few individual ship actions. Another French fleet was dispatched in 1781, strengthened by Admiral de Grasses's fleet in the Caribbean. He moved north and landed troops in the Chesapeake Bay. Sir George Rodney, commander of the British fleet, was unaware of how large the French fleet was, and he split his force, returning to Britain. This left the British fleet led by Rear Admiral Sir Thomas Graves, who engaged the French fleet of twenty-four ships of the line with his nineteen ships of the line at the Battle of the Chesapeake on 5 September 1781. The outcome was a marginal tactical victory for the French. Still, it was a strategic victory for the French and Americans that prevented the relief of Lord Cornwallis, who was besieged in Yorktown. The siege was the decisive defeat of the war and led to British recognition of the independent United States of America. Washington acknowledged to de Grasse the importance of his role in the victory: 'You will have observed that, whatever efforts are made by the land armies, the navy must have the casting vote in the present contest.'

Ambuscade's role in the war was primarily countering American privateers and interdicting supplies. US naval records list prizes taken by *Ambuscade* as part of a detached squadron operating off the Massachusetts coast.[13] On 1 October 1777, *Ambuscade* captured *St. W. Erskine,* commanded by Captain Montgomery. It was owned by Wilson and Co. in Glasgow, which possibly means it was either trading with the Americans or leased to an American firm. It is listed as a prize rather than as retaken. In June 1778, she captured the sloop *2 Brothers* commanded by Captain Maxwell. In September 1778, she recaptured *Restoration* in Boston Bay. There are also references to the capture of merchant brigs *Mary* and *Charming*

---

[13] Naval Documents of The American Revolution, Volume 11, (US Government printing office).

Sally. All of these would have been captured without much of a struggle, as *Ambuscade* massively outgunned merchant ships of this size. If the merchant ship could not outsail the frigate, they would surrender after a warning shot.

Captain the Hon. Charles Phipps by Thomas Gainsborough (Public domain)

In January 1779, Captain Thomas Haynes briefly took command of Ambuscade while she returned to Britain for repairs at Chatham Dockyard. She was recommissioned under the command of Captain the Hon. Charles Phipps in March 1779. He had been commissioned as a lieutenant in 1771 and had commanded several sixth-rate frigates, including Perseus (20), Ariel (20) and Lizard (28) in America. In February 1779, he was elected the MP for Scarborough, but he would be somewhat busy at sea for the next few years, limiting his time for politics.

On 22 June 1779, in European waters, *Ambuscade* captured the French corvette *Hélène* (16) after a short fight off Ushant. This ship had been purchased by the Royal Navy as a brig in 1778 but was captured by the French in September of that year. She was recommissioned as the schooner *Helena* (14). Six days later, *Ambuscade* captured the French privateer *Le Prince de Montbray* (20), commanded by Captain Boisnard-Maisonneuve, out of Granville, a port in Normandy.[14] She had sixteen 6-pdr and four 3-pdr guns.

---

[14]Some sources indicate that the Prince de Montbray capture came first, but we have used the order implied in the Gazette.

NOtice is hereby given to the Officers and Company of His Majesty's Ship Ambuscade, the Honourable Charles Phipps Commander, who were actually on Board the 22d and 28th of June, 1779, at taking the Helena French Brig, and Le Prince de Montbarey Privateer, that they will be paid their respective Shares of Head-money for the said Captures, on Board the Ambuscade at Portsmouth, on Friday the 7th of January, 1780; and the Sums remaining unpaid will be recalled at No. 10, America-square, Crutched-friars, London, the First Thursday in every Month for Three Years to come.

Peter Osborn,
Edward Ommanney, } *of London, Agents.*

London Gazette, 28 December 1779

In September 1779, *Ambuscade* was sent as part of a relief force to the Channel island of Guernsey, under blockade by the French. Guernsey was a notorious base for British privateers during the American Revolutionary War. Guernsey and Alderney privateers took 221 prizes worth £981,300 (about £100m today). Many Islanders bought a share in privateer ships and became rich without ever setting foot on a sailing vessel.

Ambuscade then returned to patrol duties in the Channel Fleet under Sir Francis Geary, and on 4 July 1780, she captured the American privateer *Elenore* in the North Sea.

Vice-Admiral Lord Hugh Seymour, 1759-1801 by John Hoppner (Public domain).

Captain Hugh Seymour Conway took command of *Ambuscade* in July 1780. He was commissioned in 1776 and made captain in 1779. He had commanded frigates and ships of the line before transferring to *Ambuscade*, serving in the Channel

Fleet. Meanwhile, the Spanish had entered the war with the primary aim of recapturing Gibraltar. From 1779, the Spanish bombarded and blockaded the Rock in what was called the Great Siege of Gibraltar, although several assaults were repulsed. The garrison could only be supplied by sea, requiring a fleet to break the naval blockade. There were three relief fleets in all, and Gibraltar held out until the war's end. Conway had commanded HMS *Porcupine* (24) at the first relief and at the Battle of Cape St Vincent (16 January 1780), which drove away the Spanish fleet. In the winter of 1781, *Ambuscade* would return from America to assist with the second relief of the siege. Conway would later return again to the siege, commanding the frigate HMS *Latona* (38).

Conway was not only well connected, including a friendship with the Prince of Wales, but he also had a reputation as a highly competent naval officer. He was later awarded a commemorative medal for his actions at the Battle of the Glorious First of June (1 June 1794) and is credited with introducing epaulettes to Royal Navy uniforms. He ended his career as a Vice-Admiral, commanding in the West Indies, where he contracted yellow fever and died in 1801.

Henry Duncan. Annals: North British Society, (Public Domain)

The next captain of *Ambuscade* was Henry Duncan, who transferred to the ship on 25 October 1781. He had captained HMS *Medea* (28) at the Battle of Cape Henry and the Battle of Chesapeake in America and was flag captain on HMS *Eagle* (64). This appears to have been a relatively quiet period in the war, although he obviously performed well enough to be appointed captain of HMS *Victory* (100) in April 1782. Duncan later held several senior administrative posts, including Deputy-Comptroller of the Navy, before he died in 1814.

1809 caricature of William Young while commander at Plymouth, by Robert Dighton

In April 1782, Captain William Young took command of *Ambuscade*. As part of the Downs squadron, the ship captured the privateer *Le Commander de Dunkerque* in May, *Les Petits Gens d'Armes* on 27 June, and the 13-gun Dunkirk privateer *La Middlebourg* on 28 June. None of these privateers were a match for the fighting power of *Ambuscade*, but the real skill on display was the seamanship required to catch these fast ships. Young was another *Ambuscade* captain who went on to greater things. During the French Revolutionary Wars, he captained HMS *Fortitude* (74) in several engagements and was appointed rear admiral in June 1795. Later that year, he was appointed as a Lord Commissioner of the Admiralty. He was involved in conciliating a solution to the Spithead Mutiny in April 1797, a largely successful strike by sailors to address economic grievances. Privately, he appears to have been sympathetic to the seamen's complaints, writing to a friend that 'a sad want of energy and of particular attention to duty which the government of large bodies of men requires especially in these times and an absent or indifferent man can produce incalculable mischief'. Consequently, during his tenure at the Admiralty, he tried to improve conditions and tighten discipline. He was promoted to vice-admiral, then to full admiral commanding first at Portsmouth, and then the North Sea Fleet.

The American Revolutionary War ended with the Treaty of Paris on 3 September 1783. As British troops and ships left the USA, many Royal Navy ships were paid off (mothballed), including *Ambuscade*.

Captain Thomas Boston very briefly commanded *Ambuscade* between 24 October 1787 and 19 November 1787 while she was recommissioned. After refitting, she sailed for the Mediterranean, commanded by Captain William Henry King O'Hara. Even in peacetime, the British had interests in the Mediterranean, and a fleet was maintained there. Captain Robert Devereux Fancourt took command in December 1789, while

Sir Robert Stopford (1768–1847) by William Beechey

Ambuscade remained with the Mediterranean Fleet. He later reached flag rank as a rear admiral (1808) and vice-admiral (1810). While formally at peace, this was a period of tension between Britain and Spain caused by the seizing of a British ship trading near Vancouver Island, and known as the Nootka Crisis or the Spanish Armament. Anti-Spanish public opinion in Britain forced the government to start rebuilding the Royal Navy. Both countries dispatched fleets, but they did not engage. France was allied with Spain, but as the French Revolution was breaking out, they refused to support Spain, who negotiated a peace in October 1790.

Fancourt was replaced by Acting Captain Robert Stopford on 5 December 1789, who commanded until Ambuscade was again paid off in September 1791. He was made post-captain shortly afterwards and went on to have an illustrious career in the Royal Navy, finishing his sea service as Admiral of the Red. He was still leading a British fleet into his seventies during the Syrian War of 1839.

French Revolutionary Wars

The French Revolutionary Wars were a series of conflicts lasting from 1792 until 1802. They resulted from the French Revolution that started in 1789, caused by a range of social, political and economic circumstances that the *Ancient Régime* of Louis XVI could not contain, leading to his execution. A people seeking 'liberté, égalité, and fraternité' revolutionised European politics and brought new ways of making war, on land at least. The other monarchies of Europe were outraged, and they considered whether they should intervene, either to support Louis XVI, to prevent the spread of revolution or to take strategic advantage of the chaos in France. The resulting wars were fought as a series of European nation coalitions against France. Initially confined to Europe, the fighting gradually assumed a global dimension.

France, Great Britain, and their respective allies were the major naval powers involved in the conflict. Despite its political turmoil, France made efforts to build a strong navy but suffered from the loss of experienced officers. The wars at sea were characterised by naval blockades, battles to control trade routes and coastal raids. Notable naval battles included the Glorious First of June in 1794 and the Battle of the Nile in 1798. The Royal Navy, most famously led by Admiral Horatio Nelson, achieved significant victories against the French. The British implemented a strategy known as the 'Continental Blockade' to isolate France and disrupt its trade. This severely impacted the French economy and contributed to the overall war effort. Privateers also harassed enemy shipping and contributed to the economic warfare of the period.

The Royal Navy was Britain's primary tool for what today we would call power projection, and it usually took precedence in resource allocation. It was easily the most successful force of its era, with only one ship of the line lost and not retaken, compared to the French navy's loss of ninety ships. At its maximum strength in 1810, it deployed 152 ships of the line and 183 cruisers, more than the other major naval powers combined. It was distributed in fleets worldwide, defending Britain's growing empire and threatening its enemies' trading routes. However, the navy had challenges, not least a shortage of good timber to build ships and sailors to operate them. A Royal Navy ship of this period had a diverse crew of many nationalities, not all of whom were there voluntarily. As Brian Lavery puts it, 'The Royal Navy of 1793 to 1815 reflected the society which created it. Life in the navy was hard, punishments were cruel, and death was never far away. The navy also reflected the morals and values of British culture – the class system, the political ethos, and the ambiguous attitudes to liberty.'

At the outset of the Revolutionary Wars, 32-gun frigates like *Ambuscade*, mostly armed with 12-pdr guns, were standard. However, frigates became larger as the war progressed with heavier 18- and then 24-pdr guns and carronades. They also began carrying more guns, with thirty-two, thirty-six, thirty-eight, and finally, forty guns. Many frigates in service with the Royal Navy had been captured from the enemy, including 143 from the French during the Revolutionary Wars alone. In 1801, a third of Royal Navy frigates were foreign-built. Not all prizes were taken at sea. Royal Navy ships would launch boats and sail them into harbours to cut out enemy vessels. Boats were traditionally hoisted back aboard using tackles, but this was cumbersome and slow. By the late 1790s, davits were fitted on larger ships for hoisting lighter boats, allowing them to be lifted more easily and quickly. Frigates had several quarter-boats as well as a larger launch. Carronades were mounted in them, and seamen trained in the use of small arms operated them, while marines provided the disciplined firepower.

Captain George Duff (1764–1805) by Henry Raeburn

War created a demand for more ships, particularly frigates, that could perform various functions. In May 1793, *Ambuscade* started a refit and was recommissioned in September 1794, commanded by Captain George Duff. He was born in Banff, Scotland, and had a passion for the sea, stowing away on a merchant ship for a voyage when not yet a teenager. At thirteen, he joined his great uncle, Captain (later Admiral) Robert Duff, in the Mediterranean. He was commissioned lieutenant at sixteen, breaking several fleet regulations but made possible by his uncle's interest in his career. Duff saw extensive action and commanded ships of the line before joining *Ambuscade*. The ship required further repairs for most of his period in command, so he saw little action. He subsequently returned to ships of the line, commanding the inshore squadron on HMS *Mars* (74), blockading Cadiz before the Battle of Trafalgar in 1805. It was a sign of Nelson's trust in Duff that he gave him this challenging command. In the subsequent battle, a French cannonball raked the quarterdeck and struck Duff at the base of the neck, severing his head. There is a memorial to him in the crypt of St Paul's Cathedral in London, next to Nelson's tomb. Two Second World War frigates were named after him.

In May 1796, *Ambuscade* was dispatched to the West Indies, commanded by Captain Thomas Twysden. He had been commissioned as a lieutenant in 1781, previously commanding HMS *Eurydice* (24). While there, they captured the French privateer schooner *Le Buonaparte* on 4 June 1796. He transferred to HMS *Canada* (74) in September 1797 and later died at sea off Newfoundland while commanding the former French frigate HMS *Revolutionaire* (36) in 1801.

In 1798, *Ambuscade* returned to home waters, commanded by Captain Henry Jenkins. He was commissioned as a lieutenant in 1780 and commanded HMS *Carnatic* (74) before transferring to *Ambuscade*. His command started well with the capture of the French corvette *L'Hirondelle* in the Channel on 20 November 1798. HMS *Stag* (32) and HMS *Phaeton* (38) also participated in this action.

On 14 December 1798, *Ambuscade* cruised off the Gironde in southwest France. What happened next was described by William Clowes, a naval historian of the time, as 'one of the very few actions in this war which are disgraceful to the British arms.' Captain Jenkins was expecting to be joined on this station by HMS *Stag* (32), and when a sail was sighted, he assumed this was that ship. He didn't exchange signals to confirm the vessel's identity, and the crew went to breakfast. At 9 a.m., when the ship came almost within gunshot range, she put on sail and moved away. The ship was the French corvette *Bayonnaise* (28), commanded by Lieutenant Richer. Having discovered his mistake, Jenkins gave chase, and the two ships fought for an hour. One of *Ambuscade*'s 12-pdr guns burst, damaging the ship and wounding eleven crewmen. The French ship took advantage of the confusion to break off but was caught again by *Ambuscade*. Clowes takes up the story:

'The French had so far suffered severely. At that juncture they determined to board. They had a much larger crew than had the *Ambuscade*; and serving in the Bayonnaise were thirty veteran soldiers of the Alsace regiment. The French ship ran on board the *Ambuscade*, which was becalmed as the French ship wore under her stem, carrying away the tiller ropes, starboard quarter-deck bulwarks, mizen shrouds and mizen-mast, and locking the wheel with her sprit-sail yard, and then dropped under the British vessel's stern, but did not clear her. The French soldiers from the Bayonnaise's bowsprit swept the *Ambuscade*'s deck, which was not barricaded with hammocks, with a deadly fire. In a few minutes five officers were killed or wounded in quick succession, and the command devolved upon the Purser, Mr. William Bowman Murray. An explosion of cartridges, left on the rudder-head, blew out a portion of the *Ambuscade*'s stern, and caused panic amongst her men. Most of the British crew left their quarters. At that moment, the French boarders rushed onto the *Ambuscade*'s deck and carried it.'[15]

Clowes quotes a source that claimed the British crew was 'an ill-disciplined one, and Captain Jenkins a most indiscreet and incompetent officer.' He does accept that bad management was attended by bad luck. The two explosions and the great weakness of the British crew, from which not less than thirty-one officers and men had been detached and placed on board a prize, must be taken into account. All the French officers except two were wounded; all the British executive officers were killed or wounded. The subsequent court martial acquitted Captain Jenkins and his officers for having their ship captured. They accepted that this was 'occasioned by a most rapid succession of unfortunate events: by having the mizzen-mast carried away by the enemy's bowsprit — by the wheel

---

[15] W. Clowes, The Royal Navy: A History from the Earliest Times to the Present Vol IV, (London, S. Low, Marston and Company, 1897. Digitised by University of California Libraries), pp. 516-518.

being rendered useless, and the tiller ropes broken—by the bursting of a gun, which wounded 11 men — by the blowing up of some powder and cartridges, which blew out the stern of the ship.' They also referenced the captain being wounded along with other officers and the small crew. They censured some of the crew but paid credit to the heroics of others, including Mr. Penny, a midshipman about fifteen years old.

The rare capture of a Royal Navy ship during this period was a major propaganda coup for the French. Picher and his officers were all promoted, and Major Henri Louis Lerch was made Chevalier de la Légion d'honneur for his action during the boarding. Several paintings of the event were subsequently commissioned, including a large artwork by Louis-Philippe Crépin, now one of the main exhibits of the Musée National de la Marine in Paris. *Ambuscade* was repaired and taken into French service as *L'Embuscade*.

Bayonnaise v Ambuscade by Louis-Philippe Crépin,

With *Ambuscade* renamed in French service, the name was given to a captured French frigate, *Embuscade*, on 12 October 1798. This was a

32-gun frigate launched in September 1789 at Rochefort, which had fought off the American coast before returning to France in 1795 to participate in the Croisière du Grand Hiver (Campaign of the Great Winter). This was a cruise by a French fleet from Brest that captured merchant shipping but suffered heavy losses due to sea damage. *Embuscade* was captured at the Battle of Tory Island (off Donegal) on 12 October 1798, when a French squadron attempted to land troops supporting the rebellion in Ireland.[16]

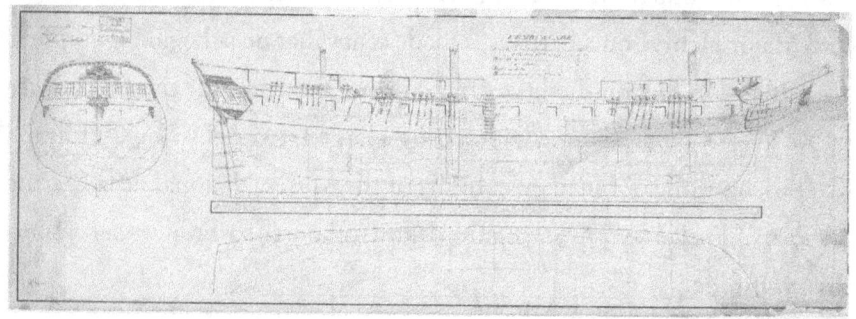

HMS Ambuscade 1798, (Royal Museums Greenwich Ship Plans 1800.)

The renamed HMS *Ambuscade* was commissioned in August 1800 as a 36-gun frigate, with twenty-six 12-pdr, eight 32-pdr, and two 6-pdr British guns, plus eight carronades. It was commanded by Captain John Colville, who had previously commanded the 16-gun sloop HMS *Star*. He was born on 15 March 1768, the second son of the 8th Lord Colville of Culross. He served in the American Revolutionary War, seeing action at Quebec in 1776 and the Battle of the Saintes in 1782. Colville reached the rank of vice-admiral and succeeded to the title due to the death of his older brother.

Ambuscade initially served in home waters, based at Plymouth. In 1801, she was sent to Jamaica on convoy duty. On the return journey, she

---

[16]TNA, Court of Admiralty papers, HCA 32:516

fought off French frigates bound for Saint-Domingue. She was paid off at Sheerness in September 1802.

There was also another very short-lived HMS *Ambuscade* in this period. The 32-gun Dutch frigate *Embuscade* was captured by the Royal Navy on 30 August 1799. She foundered on 9 July 1801 at Sheerness but was salvaged. Initially she was added as *Ambuscade*, but was renamed *Helder* on 25 March 1803 before entering service with the Royal Navy.

In 1802, the British and French signed the Treaty of Amiens, ending the war. The peace held for less than a year but still constituted the longest period of peace between the two countries during the period 1793-1815. The treaty marks the transition between the French Revolutionary Wars and the Napoleonic Wars, although Napoleon was not crowned emperor until 1804.

Those who also served

Sir Patrick Campbell

Not every officer serving on *Ambuscade* was born into the service. Patrick Campbell was born in Argyll in 1773 into an army family and went to sea in 1788 as a captain's servant. He was promoted to midshipman in 1790 and served on *Ambuscade* between January 1791 and July 1792. He went on to serve on many ships in the Mediterranean and English Channel, taking part in several small ship actions and was successful in every one, even surviving a double shipwreck in 1805. He finished the Napoleonic Wars as the captain of HMS *Leviathan* (74) and was knighted in 1815. He returned to the service in 1814 and was appointed rear admiral in 1830.

John Ballantyne

John Ballantyne entered the Royal Navy in 1794 as an able seaman. He served as master's mate on *Ambuscade* for over five years between 1799 and 1805. He was commissioned as a lieutenant in 1807 and served on several small ships until the end of the Napoleonic Wars.

Henry Curzon

Henry Curzon was the fifth son of the 1st Baron Scarsdale and joined the Royal Navy in 1776, serving four years as an able seaman. He was commissioned in 1783 and served on *Ambuscade* between 1787 and 1788 as a second lieutenant. He fought in almost every theatre of war from India to Canada and the East Indies. He reached the rank of admiral in 1830.

The Soldier and his Wife resting themselves at the Second Mile Stone.

William Webster, a nineteen-year-old officer on *Ambuscade* who was originally from Dundee, kept a private diary of his service on the ship in 1795-6. During this time, *Ambuscade* was undertaking convoy escort duties to Denmark. Webster had time ashore in Denmark, dining with the family of the butcher that supplied meat to the ship. He was a keen observer of everyday life, and his diary is illustrated by many sketches. The ability to sketch and draw maps was an important skill for an officer in days long before the mobile phone camera. Webster described the city of Copenhagen in detail and wrote enthusiastically back to his uncle, who appears to have brought him up as a child, saying, 'You have frequently told me that novices often pay too much for their experience. So has been my case.' His journal later got him briefly arrested, as the Danish authorities thought he was spying.[17]

The Napoleonic Wars

Peace was short-lived, with Britain declaring war on France on 18 May 1803. It was joined in 1804-5 by the Third Coalition, comprised of the United Kingdom, the Austrian Empire, the Russian Empire, Naples, Sicily, and Sweden. The war on land went badly, with a swift French victory in the Ulm Campaign (October 1805) that captured an entire Austrian army, and the decisive French victory over a combined Austro-Russian force at the Battle of Austerlitz in December 1805. Austerlitz brought the Third Coalition to an end. The wars continued with a series of coalitions against the French, with Britain as the consistent foe, culminating in the Battle of Waterloo in 1815.

At sea, the Royal Navy had its most famous victory at the Battle of Trafalgar on 21 October 1805, when Admiral Nelson defeated the combined French and Spanish fleets off the coast of Spain. Nelson was mortally wounded in the battle, but the action ensured that the Royal Navy dominated the seas for the rest of the Napoleonic Wars.

---

[17] Diary of William Webster Officer Ambuscade 1795-96, (National Maritime Museum, Greenwich)

The Battle of Trafalgar by Nicholas Pocock (Public domain)

Control of the seas kept the Royal Navy busy throughout this period, fighting worldwide and not always successfully, such as the attempt to capture Istanbul in 1807. The most common operation was blockading the French coast in the English Channel and the Mediterranean—a thankless and arduous task even in the best weather. Squadrons were dispatched around the world to the Adriatic, West Indies, South Africa, and the East Indies. There was even a war against the USA between 1812–15, which involved actions off the American coast as well as on the Great Lakes when the USA invaded Canada. In August 1814, British ships landed troops that marched to Washington and burned the White House in retaliation for an American attack on York in Canada.

While the significant battles were fought by ships of the line, frigates were the eyes and ears of the fleet. They were also dispatched singly or in squadrons to anywhere in the world. Admirals could never get enough frigates for all the tasks they required. When Nelson was chasing the French fleet around the Mediterranean, he cried, '*Were I to die this moment, want of frigates would be found engraved on my heart!*'

While most histories focus on the great sea battles of the period, convoy protection was the main role of most Royal Navy ships, defending the trade that provided the sinews of war, and moving troops to the continent and beyond. Without convoys, and the frigates like *Ambuscade* to protect them, Britain could not have emerged victorious from the war. The significance of convoys in securing essential resources cannot be overstated. Bullion from Mexico, coffee and sugar from the tropics, and foodstuffs were crucial for financing the war and keeping the armies and population fed. Saltpetre from Bengal and sulphur from Sicily were vital for making the gunpowder with which the army fought. They also transported more exotic cargo, such as four kangaroos to St Petersburg as a present from King George to Emperor Alexander. What the kangaroos made of being taken from Australia to the Russian winter is not recorded! The importance of convoys was largely forgotten after the Napoleonic Wars, only to be reinstated in 1917 when U-boat losses became unsustainable. In World War II, the convoy system played an equally crucial role in securing victory.

At the outset of renewed hostilities, *Ambuscade* was commanded by Captain David Colby, having been the flagship for Rear Admiral Edward Thornbrough in the North Sea. Colby had been wounded at the Battle of the Glorious First of June in 1794 before returning to command the frigate HMS *Dido* (16). After *Ambuscade,* he commanded four ships of the line, finishing as the captain of HMS *Royal Sovereign* (100) in 1809.

On 28 May 1803, the original *Ambuscade*, now the French frigate *L'Embuscade,* returned to our story. Returning to France from the West Indies with a depleted crew and some damage, she met with HMS *Victory* near Rochefort. HMS *Victory* was on her way to the Mediterranean to become Nelson's famous flagship. *L'Embuscade* tried to escape, but HMS *Victory*, despite her age, was a fast ship of the line and, with one hundred guns, massively outgunned the frigate. She surrendered without firing a shot and was taken to Portsmouth.

She was recommissioned into the Royal Navy as a 32-gun frigate *Ambuscade* in 1804. However, it appears that she undertook some patrols while being refitted at Sheerness and at the Nore. These included cruising off the coast of Holland and convoy escort duties.[18] The previously French *Ambuscade* was renamed as HMS *Seine*. She served in the West Indies and home waters, capturing seven French and Spanish ships before being broken up in 1813.

Back in Royal Navy service, *Ambuscade* was commanded by Captain William Durban (the proper spelling is D'Urban, but it was misspelt in his passing certificate). He had previously served in the West Indies and the Mediterranean and, after the Revolutionary Wars, commanded HMS *Weazle* (16) based in Jersey. He was sent to the Mediterranean with news of the Peace of Amiens and was crucial in persuading the Knights of Malta not to surrender the Order to France. Subsequently, he was used for several diplomatic missions in the region. With Nelson's support, he was promoted to command *Ambuscade*. He continued to be used in various special service roles across the Mediterranean, with few opportunities to benefit from the prize money enjoyed by other frigate captains on this station. The ship's log describes these journeys (although, sadly, not the details of the missions) around the coast of Italy and Sicily, including stops in Malta and Naples. Durban clearly ran a tight ship, with not untypical levels of discipline. The ship's log records on 23 September 1805, punishment for Lewis Edwards with twenty-nine lashes for contempt; two other seamen received twelve lashes for drunkenness, another got twenty-nine lashes for disobedience and two others received twenty-four lashes for sleeping on their watch.[19]

---

[18] TNA, Letters from Captains 1801-04, ADM 1/1450
[19] TNA, Journal, HMS Ambuscade 1805, Captain Durban, ADM 51:1533.

> Moderate breezes, made & shortened sail occly, at 9 wore Ship, AM at 1 Tacked, employed working up Junk, unbent Sheet Cable. boarded an Imperial from Constantinople to Leghorn, Punished Lewis Edwards (S) with 29 lashes for Contempt, Benj. Parkinson & Jn° Palmer with 12 lashes each for Drunkness, Jn° Cloughli with 29 Lashes for Disobed.t of Orders, Jas. Allen & Dan.l Workman (Mr) with 24 Lashes each for Sleeping on their watch. —

The Royal Naval Biography describes his service:

'Having thus given an outline of Captain D'Urban's valuable services, it remains only for us to state that there is perhaps no individual who possesses so much local knowledge of the Mediterranean as he obtained during upwards of twelve years spent on that station, or who is so intimately acquainted with the manners, customs, and prejudices of the different nations on both its shores as himself. It was on this account that Nelson and his successor, Collingwood, as also other superior officers employed him frequently as a negotiator on matters of so secret a nature that it would be impolitic even now to make them public, particularly one mission relating to the Venetian Government. Although his services have not been of that brilliant cast with those of many whose exploits we have recorded, yet they have nevertheless proved in many instances highly beneficial to his country, and as such gained him the thanks and esteem of all the Admirals he ever served under, although, at the same time they deprived him of cruises, the advantages of which were reaped by the mere sailor, who is now enjoying his golden harvest, while the labours of his more scientific contemporary, are in a great measure forgotten.'[20]

The master's log for *Ambuscade* during this period gives another perspective to life aboard the ship. As with the ship's log, it records the

---

[20] J. Marshall, d'Urban, William, (Royal Naval Biography), https://en.m.wikisource.org/wiki/Royal_Naval_Biography/d%27Urban,_William

position of the ship, wind and weather and any notable events. The master also records supplies. For example, in 1805 the master was Alex Cannon, and he recorded a delivery of supplies on 1 November 1805 at Malta that included 915 gallons of wine. There was also lemon juice, which was used to treat and prevent scurvy. This was discovered aboard HMS *Salisbury* in 1747 by Dr James Lind, although it is not clear why the Royal Navy waited forty-two years before making this a requirement.[21] Dr Lind is remembered today as the father of naval medicine.

While *Ambuscade* was not regularly cruising for enemy ships, the master's log does record interceptions of merchant ships to check if they were carrying supplies for the enemy.[22]

Ambuscade ended her Royal Navy service, broken up at Deptford in 1810.

The final *Ambuscade* of the Napoleonic Wars was formerly *Pomone*, a 40-gun *Hortense*-class frigate of the French Navy, built at Genoa for the

---

[21]M. White, 'James Lind: The man who helped to cure scurvy with lemons', (BBC, Oct. 2016), https://www.bbc.co.uk/news/uk-england-37320399
[22]TNA, Master's logs Ambuscade, ADM 52/3726

Ligurian Republic. She was captured near Corfu during the action of 29 November 1811 and briefly added to the Royal Navy as *Ambuscade*, although she was never brought into service. She was broken up in November 1812 at Woolwich Dockyard.

Frigate Pomone in Toulon by Antoine Roux (Public Domain)

And that was almost it for *Ambuscade* in the age of sail. However, in May 1828, a 36-gun sail-powered frigate was ordered from Woolwich Dockyard as *Ambuscade*. Sadly, she was renamed in March 1831 as HMS *Amphion* and then redesigned as a screw-propelled frigate. Launched in 1846, HMS *Amphion* served in the Baltic Sea during the Crimean War against Russia before being broken up in 1863. *Ambuscade* could not be described as a lucky ship during the Revolutionary and Napoleonic Wars, and their Lordships probably decided that *Amphion*, which won the Battle of Lissa in 1811 under Sir William Hoste, was perhaps a safer name for a new type of warship.

Nevertheless, *Ambuscade* and her sister frigates served the Royal Navy well during the age of sail. They could carry provisions for six months, allowing them to sail anywhere in the world without visiting a port—the equivalent of a nuclear-powered ship of today. Frigates also became a growing element of the Royal Navy, from 15 per cent of warship tonnage in 1710 to 43 per cent in 1810.[23] British shipyards built five hundred warships and six thousand merchant ships during the war, and prizes were taken from enemy states. They were needed because French privateers captured 5,314 ships between 1803 and 1814. However, winter weather caused more casualties than enemy action. Sixty-one per cent of warship losses were due to the weather.

As Napoleon said, *'Wherever you find a fathom of water, there you will find the British.'* And we should also say thank you to the quite exceptional officers and crew who served in them.

---

[23]D. Baugh, The Oxford Illustrated History of the Royal Navy, (Oxford, 1995), p.124.

CHAPTER THREE: THE FIRST WORLD WAR

During the age of sail, the ships named HMS *Ambuscade* were frigates whose tasks included being the eyes of the fleet, escorting, and raiding commerce. By the late nineteenth century, warship design had evolved considerably with armoured steamships, rifled guns and the self-propelled torpedo. It was the torpedo that would enable smaller ships to take on ships of the line in battle for the first time.

Robert Whitehead developed the first self-propelled torpedo from an initial design by Giovanni Luppis for the Austro-Hungarian navy. Whitehead was born in Bolton but made his name while working in Fiume (modern Rijeka in Croatia) when he was asked to develop the Luppis design. He built two types of torpedoes for the world's navies, powered by compressed air and carrying an explosive warhead. By the 1870s, his torpedo could travel at seven knots and hit a target seven hundred yards away.

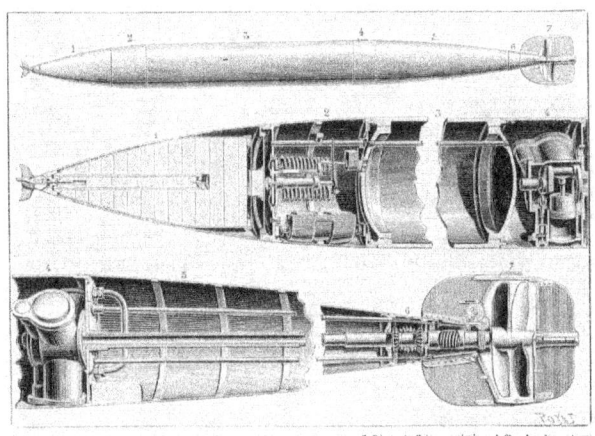

The Whitehead Torpedo mechanism 1891 (Louis Poyet, Public domain)

This torpedo was probably first used in combat during the Russo-Turkish War when, on 16 January 1878, the Ottoman ship *Intibah* was sunk by Russian torpedo boats carrying Whiteheads.[24] The Royal Navy bought manufacturing rights in 1871, and Whitehead opened a test site in Portland Harbour, Dorset, in 1890. On retirement, he sold the company to the British armaments companies Vickers and Armstrong-Whitworth. By this time, most of the world's navies had started to respond to the torpedo, with ships being sunk by torpedoes in several conflicts. Some naval theorists predicted the torpedo would end the role of the armoured battleship; although this theory proved misplaced, the torpedo did lead to a range of countermeasures.

There is a room dedicated to the Whitehead torpedo in the Croatian Naval Museum, Split (Author)

---

[24] At least one source contests this. See R. Stem, Destroyer Battles: Epics of Naval Close Combat, (Pen & Sword) pp. 18–19.

The Royal Navy issued a specification to private firms in 1892 to design a new class of ships called 'torpedo boat destroyers', known as 'destroyers' in common parlance before the term was officially adopted. The leading shipbuilding firms, including Yarrows on the Clyde, built six prototypes that were taken into service. They had long, narrow hulls, with a torpedo tube (14-inch and later 18-inch) at the front and a 12-pdr quick-firing gun above the conning tower. The maximum torpedo range was 500 yards, although the chances of hitting anything at that range were remote. Life for the crew aboard an early destroyer was tough, and crews were awarded a special allowance for serving on them. They also developed a more relaxed ethos compared to the highly regimented atmosphere in the rest of the Royal Navy.

As torpedoes' range, speed, and stability improved, the Royal Navy saw the opportunity to develop destroyers as part of the battle fleet at sea. The new destroyers had to be large enough to operate with the fleet in all weather. They carried 18-inch and then 21-inch torpedoes, capable of attacking from a range of between 3,800 yards and 10,000 yards, depending on the speed. However, the chances of hitting a moving ship at those ranges were remote. Thirty-nine *River*-class destroyers were built between 1903 and 1905 to meet this need. Germany was rapidly building a more extensive fleet, and their own design, the *S90*, preempted the British launch in 1900. By 1907, the Royal Navy was building the larger *Tribal* class, which was faster and more heavily armed, in response to the revolutionary battleship design known as dreadnoughts.

From 1907, the Royal Navy commissioned three types of destroyers. Coastal destroyers which were cheap but slow; fleet destroyers capable of operating with the battle fleet; and flotilla leaders which were large, fast destroyers with accommodation for the flotilla commander. Each destroyer class had a letter designation, G to W classes, and were typically armed with two (later three) 4-inch guns, two 12-pdr guns and two 21-inch torpedoes. The *Acasta* class developed from a 1910 Admiralty specification for a torpedo boat destroyer with quick-firing guns, speed, seaworthiness, low cost and good radius. They doubted a destroyer could manage more than thirty knots in North Sea conditions, even though foreign navies were building large destroyers capable of higher speeds. The final *Acasta* designs were larger and heavier armed than the preceding H and I classes, displacing about 25 per cent more, and the mixed calibre armament was replaced with a uniform fit of quick-firing 4-inch guns. Twelve vessels were built to a common Admiralty design, including *Ambuscade*, along with eight builders' specials with small variations in design.

HMS *Ambuscade*

Ambuscade was built as an *Acasta*-class destroyer (later becoming the K class) at John Browns, Clydebank, as part of the 1911-12 shipbuilding programme. Her overall length was 276 feet, 6 inches (81.5m), with a beam of 27 feet (8.2m) and a draught of 10 feet, 6 inches (3.2m). The ship was powered by Yarrow-type water-tube boilers and Brown-Curtis steam turbines, generating 29 knots (33 mph). She was armed with three quick-firing 4-inch guns (120 shells per gun), and two 21-inch torpedo tubes with two reload torpedoes. Later in the war, a 2-pdr 'pom-pom' anti-aircraft gun was fitted along with depth charges. It was fuelled by oil in four tanks with a capacity of 47,910 gallons, giving it an optimum range of 1,540 nautical miles (1,772 land miles).

HMS Ambuscade with insert pictures of the King and Admiral Jellico (Author's collection)

Coles, Gordon Alston (IWM Lives of WW1)

She was launched on 25 January 1913 and commissioned in June of the same year. Her first commander was Lieutenant-Commander Gordon Alston Coles. He was born in India, where his father was Director General of Prisons. The young Coles was sent to Britannia Naval College, Dartmouth and passed out in July 1897. Naval cadets generally came from professional middle-class families who could afford to pay the £50 per year (£8,000 at 2023 prices) additional allowance to supplement the modest 'navy pay'. The education was of a high standard in traditional subjects with the addition of navigation and seamanship. Discipline was strict, with independent thinking often brutally repressed, but it generated tough sailors physically and mentally. Coles was commissioned as a lieutenant in 1903 and commanded the destroyer HMS *Boxer* from 1910. He was promoted to lieutenant-commander in 1911 before transferring to *Ambuscade*. He moved to the new M-class destroyer HMS *Plucky* in July 1916 and was promoted to commander in December of that year. He ended the war, commanding the Fourth Flotilla of Fish Hydrophone Trawlers, then the battleship HMS *Agamemnon* in 1919. He was still on the retired list at the rank of captain during the Second World War and died in 1971.

Destroyers in this period were usually commanded, not by a captain as with the previous *Ambuscades*, but by a lieutenant-commander. This rank in the Royal Navy was introduced in March 1914, to which lieutenants of eight years' seniority were promoted. It was an evolved form of the 'lieutenant & commander' designation or 'lieutenant in command' used in Navy lists before its institution. Lieutenant-commanders wore two rows of one-half inch gold lace on their sleeves, with a row of one-quarter inch lace between them. On their full-dress uniforms, a fouled anchor was worn below a star on epaulettes.

Coles commanded a crew of seventy-four.[25] Destroyers did not have their own paymaster, so precise dates of service on the ship were not always accurate. Crew members could be moved around the ships in the flotilla. There was a small complement of officers, including the second-in-command, initially Lieutenant Irving Palmer, later Lieutenant Eric Davis (joined August 1915) and Sub-Lieutenant Alan Boyle De Blaquiere (joined November 1915). There was also a surgeon-lieutenant or probationer, typically a medical student who had passed their second-year exam in anatomy and physiology. Learning on the job took on a whole new meaning during wartime. Finally, there was a torpedo gunner, Thomas 'Paddy' Lynch, who was replaced by Evelyn Leppan in May 1916. The officers' quarters were at the rear of the ship and were relatively spacious, with their own cabin and shared wardroom facilities. There was a shared toilet and a portable tin bath in each cabin.

---

[25]HMS Ambuscade crew list at Jutland, https://battleofjutlandcrewlists.miraheze.org/wiki/HMS_Ambuscade_Crew_List

Crew quarters for the ratings were positioned forward in cramped, unhealthy conditions. The crew generally slept ashore in the early destroyers, but that wasn't an option for fleet destroyers. Oil-fired destroyers were at least cleaner than coal-fired ships, but they were still damp and poorly ventilated. Condensation poured down the side of the mess deck walls, making any attempt to keep dry difficult. Washing facilities were limited to just four washbasins, and showers consisted of seawater poured over the rating from a bucket. OK, in summer, but not an attractive prospect in winter. There were no laundry facilities, which meant clothes were washed, if at all, in a bucket. Day to day command of ratings was undertaken by the chief petty officer (known as 'the jaunty') and his petty officers. They had a separate mess, while the remaining crew messed in groups of between twenty and thirty men in a space the size of an average modern house lounge, which served as a combined bedroom and dining room. Hammocks were slung over the mess tables at night for sleeping.

The working day was divided into five four-hour duty periods, starting at 8 pm to midnight, with the final 'dog watch' split into two two-hour shifts (4 pm to 6 pm and 6 pm to 8 pm). The ship's bell would sound every half hour, the number of strokes indicating the time with every eight indicating a change of watch. There were five recognised meal periods. However, the ship only had one cook's mate, who mostly cooked for the

Signalman Frank Linney joined HMS Ambuscade in January 1916. (IWM Lives of WW1)

officers and senior ratings. For the lower decks, ratings took turns acting as cooks, ironically referred to as 'chef de la maison'. Carrying the cooked food from the galley to the mess could be challenging in rough seas, with meals often ending on the deck. Service on a small ship in the stormy North Atlantic or North Sea winter seas could be hazardous. Thousands of gallons of seawater would crash along the deck, making movement treacherous. Even the most experienced ratings were frequently seasick, and disease could quickly spread in the cramped conditions.

In this period, distance signalling was done by wireless telegraphy, or Morse code, transmitted by electromagnetic waves. Telegraphists (known as 'sparkers') were trained at Devonport on a six-month course, and were required to be able to read twenty-two words per minute and transmit ten words per minute in order to pass out. They were also trained as coders. Leading Telegraphist Basil Phillips joined *Ambuscade* on 21 February 1915, and his diary formed the basis for much of Pat Avery's book, which describes life on *Ambuscade* in 1916.[26]

Winston Churchill campaigned for better pay and conditions for sailors, recognising the poor conditions on board ships. He also responded to the campaign led by Lionel Yexley, a former petty officer who edited the lower-deck monthly *The Fleet*. Yexley's strong criticism of food quality, corruption, pay and harsh punishments eventually won over the First Sea Lord, Admiral Sir John Fisher. There were no less than twenty-four recorded incidents of mutiny between 1900 and 1914.[27]

Ambuscade got off to a bad start when, on 31 July 1913, she collided with another K-class destroyer, HMS *Sparrowhawk*. A court of enquiry determined that Lieutenant-Commander Coles had handled *Ambuscade* in a 'faulty' manner.

---

[26] P. Avery, Duel in the North Sea, (Sea Funnel, 2016).
[27] Q. Barry, The War in the North Sea (Helion, 2016), p. 45.

Wartime Service

The First World War erupted on 28 July 1914 when Austria-Hungary invaded Serbia following the assassination of Archduke Franz Ferdinand. This led to a chain reaction of war declarations driven by alliances. The Allied Powers included France, the UK, Russia, Italy, and Japan, and in 1917, the USA. They fought against the Central Powers, which included Germany, Austria-Hungary, and the Ottoman Empire. The German invasion of France quickly developed into the trench warfare most associated with the conflict. Fighting on the Eastern Front was more open, flowing backwards and forwards across vast areas. There was also fighting in the Balkans, Africa and the Far East.

The naval war was fought in all these theatres, but for the Royal Navy, the focus was on the North Sea, where the Grand Fleet faced the German High Seas Fleet and blockaded Germany. For the first time, this was to be more than an observational blockade. The blockade aimed to impact Germany's economy significantly and contributed to the eventual exhaustion of German resources. The British Grand Fleet would be based at Scapa Flow in Orkney to block off the North Sea, and the Channel Fleet would close the Straits of Dover. Both sides employed dreadnoughts (heavily armed and armoured battleships), battlecruisers, and submarines. The use of naval aviation, mines and torpedoes became widespread, posing significant threats to surface vessels. The German use of U-boats (submarines), particularly with the policy of unrestricted submarine warfare, was a pivotal aspect of naval warfare. Germany employed U-boats to sink merchant and passenger ships, including those of neutral nations, without warning. This policy contributed to the United States' decision to enter the war on the Allies' side.

At the outbreak of war in 1914, *Ambuscade* was part of the Fourth Destroyer Flotilla, based initially at Portsmouth, before joining the Grand

Fleet. The flotilla consisted of twenty K-class destroyers commanded from HMS *Swift*. There was also a depot ship, HMS *Hecla*, which handled administration, minor repairs and supplies for the flotilla.

HMS Ambuscade during the First World War (Ernest Hopkins, Public domain)

Ambuscade first saw action on 16 December 1914 as part of an action against German battlecruisers bombarding the coastal towns of Scarborough, Whitby and Hartlepool. The Germans aimed to draw out units of the Grand Fleet where they could be engaged piecemeal by the High Seas Fleet. The Royal Navy sent four battlecruisers under Vice Admiral David Beatty and the six battleships of Vice Admiral Sir George Warrender's Second Battle Squadron to challenge the raiders. *Ambuscade* was one of seven destroyers screening the battlecruiser squadron, and they spotted a German destroyer (V155) screening the German fleet. HMS *Lynx* engaged the German destroyer, but a jammed propeller caused her to turn and collide with *Ambuscade*. Damaged below the waterline and heavily flooded, *Ambuscade* had to drop out of the attack. Fighting continued between elements of both fleets before the Germans withdrew, fearing they might face the whole Grand Fleet.

After repairs, *Ambuscade* rejoined the Grand Fleet. She took part in a sortie off the Danish coast on 21 April 1916, which aimed to distract attention from Russian minelaying operations in the Baltic. In heavy fog, *Ambuscade* collided with the destroyer HMS *Ardent*; *Ardent* had to be towed home. This was not the only collision during this fog-impacted sortie. Collisions also occurred between the battlecruisers *Australia* and *New Zealand* and between the battleship *Neptune* and a neutral merchant ship. The court of inquiry found that 21-year-old Sub-Lieutenant De Blaquiere, as Officer of the Watch, was chiefly responsible for *Ambuscade*'s collision due to his 'reckless and inexact orders for the use of the helm.' Admiral Jellicoe decided that De Blaquiere should be appointed to a larger ship to 'learn his duties'. However, events would intervene. *Ambuscade* was repaired at the Swan Hunter shipyard at Wallsend until 26 May, when she sailed north to rejoin the Grand Fleet at its Scapa Flow, Orkney, base.

The Battle of Jutland

The Battle of Jutland, fought from 31 May to 1 June 1916, was the largest naval battle of World War I and a crucial engagement between the Royal Navy's Grand Fleet, commanded by Admiral Sir John Jellicoe, and the German Imperial Navy's High Seas Fleet, commanded by Vice-Admiral Reinhard Scheer. The battle took place in the North Sea, near the coast of Denmark's Jutland Peninsula. The significantly smaller German fleet sought to break the blockade of Germany and challenge Britain's naval supremacy. *Ambuscade* left Scapa Flow with the ships of the 4th Flotilla on 30 May, having been ordered to screen the 3rd Battlecruiser Squadron based at Rosyth.

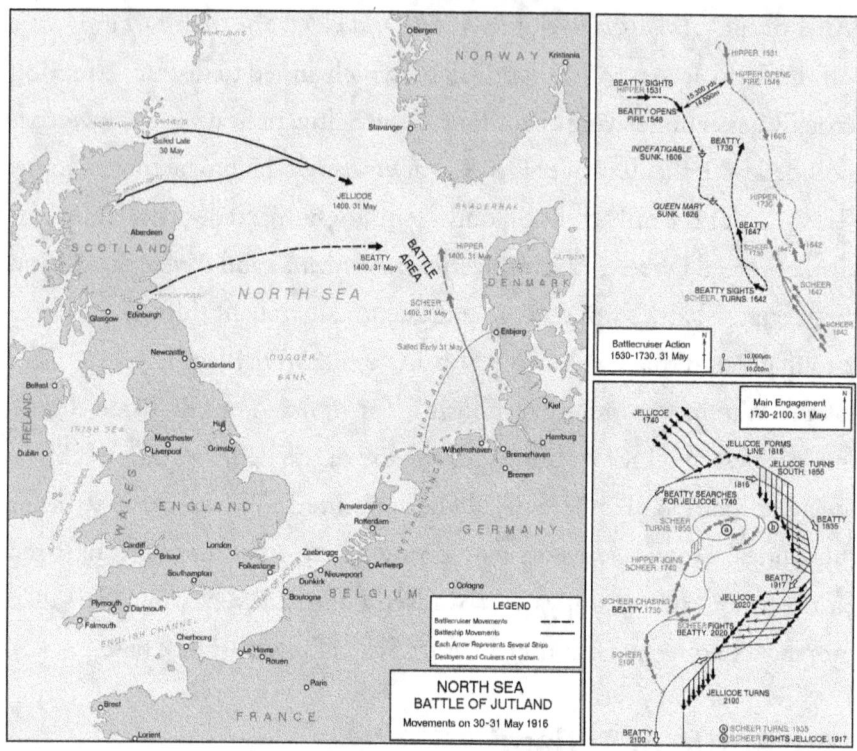

Battle of Jutland (Department of History at the United States Military Academy, Public Domain)

The battle began when British and German naval forces encountered each other on the afternoon of May 31, 1916. The initial engagement involved clashes between the opposing battlecruiser squadrons. With thinner armour, the British battlecruisers suffered significant losses, including the explosive loss of three ships: HMS *Indefatigable*, HMS *Queen Mary*, and HMS *Invincible*. The main battleship fleets joined the fight in the evening as the battle progressed. *Ambuscade* was an onlooker to the firing as she sought to reach a position ahead of the fleet. However, her Clyde-built sister ship HMS *Acasta* was hit by a ricochet 5.9-inch shell from the German battlecruiser SMS *Derfflinger*.

The night phase of the battle was characterized by confused and sporadic engagements, with both fleets manoeuvring in the dark, largely unaware of each other. *Ambuscade* was ahead of the Second Battle Squadron when they contacted a line of German battleships and cruisers. The 4th Flotilla leader, HMS *Tipperary*, was caught in German searchlights and was severely damaged, later sinking. The German ships turned away to avoid torpedo attacks from the British destroyers, with the cruiser SMS *Elbing* badly damaged in a collision with the battleship SMS *Posen*. All the British torpedoes missed their targets.

The German cruiser SMS *Rostock* was then spotted, but successfully damaged HMS *Broke* which, losing control, collided with another destroyer, HMS *Sparrowhawk*. Matters got worse when HMS *Contest* ran into *Sparrowhawk*. As *Rostock* turned away, *Ambuscade* launched a torpedo attack with both tubes, firing at high speed at around one thousand yards. One of the torpedoes hit *Rostock* on the port side between the two foremost boiler rooms. This disabled the ship, which almost collided with other German ships before the destroyer *S54* assisted them to head back to base. However, the cruiser HMS *Dublin* later found them, and *Rostock* was abandoned and deliberately torpedoed by escorting German destroyers. The remaining crew were transferred to the destroyers under cover of a smokescreen.

This wasn't the end of the battle for *Ambuscade*. The spare torpedo was loaded, a challenging proposition in the dark on a pitching sea. That torpedo was fired at a line of German ships, and although a flash was seen, it could have come from attacks by other ships in the flotilla. HMS *Achates* now led the remaining five destroyers of the flotilla, including *Ambuscade*, back towards the German battle line. Heavily outgunned by the German battleships and cruisers, two more destroyers were sunk, HMS *Fortune* and HMS *Ardent*. *Ambuscade* was now being hunted by German cruisers but managed to escape under cover of a smoke screen.

The battle overall was tactically inconclusive, with neither side achieving a decisive victory. Strategically, the British Grand Fleet managed to maintain control of the North Sea, preventing the German High Seas Fleet from breaking the blockade. Both sides suffered heavy losses, with the British losing fourteen ships and over six thousand men and the Germans losing eleven ships and around twenty-five hundred men. The 4th Flotilla had lost five ships during the battle. The post-battle review identified a lack of torpedo training prior to the battle due to the other demands on the ships. The lack of coordination in attacks and the German tactic of immediately turning away also contributed to the limited success.

Overall, the battle exposed the limitations of destroyers in a fleet encounter. Peacetime exercises suggested that 30 per cent of torpedoes would hit their targets. However, the British fired 96 torpedoes at Jutland and scored six hits. The Germans, who had even higher expectations, fired 105 and scored two, possibly three hits. Aiming a torpedo from a fast-moving ship at a target that was also moving and not on a steady course was extremely difficult. Torpedoes fired at long range could be pushed off course by propeller wash as ships turned away, the standard tactic. As Crossley puts it, 'It seems surprising in retrospect not that so few hits were obtained, but rather that anyone expected any better results.'[28] More effective was the threat of destroyer action. The mass attack by German destroyers forced the Grand Fleet to turn away at a crucial moment in the battle, and laying smoke floats made British gunfire much less effective.

Lieutenant-Commander Coles was awarded the Distinguished Service Order for his actions during the battle, and he was mentioned in despatches and recommended for early promotion. His citation read, 'The commander of his division speaks highly of the way he conned his ship. *Ambuscade* fired three torpedoes, and the rapid reloading under fire

---
[28] J. Crossley, British Destroyers 1892-1918, (Osprey, 2010), p.42.

reflects great credit on all concerned, and proves the ship is in a high state of efficiency.' The second in command, Lieutenant Eric Davis, was commended, as was Petty Officer William Wakeling. The unfortunate De Blaquiere was transferred to a larger ship, HMS *Zealandia*. However, he fared little better and was moved again. En route to his new posting in the Caribbean, his transport ship SS *Laurentic* struck a mine, sinking her with 354 crew and passengers, including De Blaquiere.

Post-Jutland service

After the battle, most of the crew transferred to HMS *Plucky*, focusing on anti-submarine warfare and convoy escort. *Ambuscade* remained in the 4th Flotilla, moving to the Humber to protect minesweepers and deterring German minelayers under Lieutenant-Commander Henry Scott. He had been commissioned as a lieutenant in 1907 and served in several destroyers before joining *Ambuscade* in June 1916. He had a less than auspicious start to the war when, on 29 August 1914, he grounded his torpedo boat in the Firth of Forth, incurring Their Lordships' displeasure 'for careless navigation & gross carelessness'. He went on to command another destroyer, HMS *Oriana,* for the remainder of the war and retired in 1931 with the rank of captain.

Raids by German torpedo boats across the Channel in October 1916 resulted in a need to strengthen the Dover Patrol. The Channel routes to France were vital in bringing troops and supplies to the armies on the Western Front. The Germans had based forty destroyers and torpedo boats in occupied Belgium to disrupt these convoys. U-boats also passed through the Channel on their way to attack Atlantic convoys. In just under three years, the Dover Patrol passed 120,000 ships across the Channel and carried 5,600,000 troops to France, with a fraction of one per cent lost to enemy action, mostly mines.

The Dover Patrol commanded a wide variety of ship types, including cruisers, monitors, destroyers, armed trawlers and drifters, paddle minesweepers, armed yachts, motor launches and coastal motor boats, submarines, seaplanes, aeroplanes and airships. There were never enough ships, particularly destroyers, to take the war to the enemy, as the Royal Navy had not expected to face German forces in Belgium. They were also low on the priority list for modern ships. This meant that older warships had to operate at sea for much longer than planned and faced German destroyers who could outpace them. The German destroyers regularly attacked the Dover Barrage, a barrier of minefields and indicator nets anchored to the sea bed between Belgium and Dover. They also undertook hit-and-run raids on coastal towns; although they did minor damage, these raids were difficult to counter.

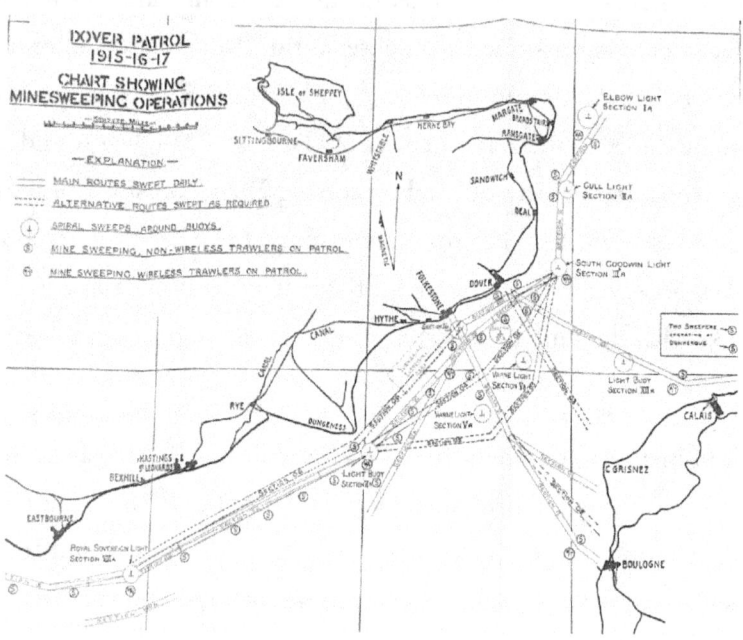

The Dover Patrol main routes across the Channel (from 'The Dover Patrol', 1919)

The 4th Flotilla was transferred to Portsmouth for anti-submarine operations. *Ambuscade* was one of five destroyers transferred from the

4th to the 6th Destroyer Flotilla, part of the Dover Patrol in November 1916. She also had a new commander, Lieutenant in Command Reginald Nash. He had been commissioned a lieutenant in 1911 and served in destroyers before transferring to *Ambuscade* on 18 October 1916. He was awarded the Distinguished Service Cross for Miscellaneous Services on 22 June 1917. He commanded other destroyers after leaving *Ambuscade* and retired in 1932 with the rank of commander.

On the Dover Patrol, *Ambuscade* was responsible for anti-submarine patrols and convoy escort work, most often with the fellow K-class destroyers HMS *Cockatrice* and HMS *Christopher*. They also defended the Dover Barrage. In March 1916, the Germans discovered they could pass on the surface at night, a weakness not fixed until August 1916 with new mines and searchlights. There were also raids on the German-held coastline and a blockade of Ostend and Zeebrugge. A close blockade was impractical because shore guns could hit destroyers at sixteen thousand yards during daylight and eight thousand yards at night.

On 4 April 1917, *Ambuscade* left the 6th Flotilla, with *Cockatrice* and *Christopher*, to rejoin the 4th Flotilla, now based at Devonport. Nash left *Ambuscade* in November 1917 and was replaced by Lieutenant in Command Maxwell Ritter. He was commissioned lieutenant in 1913 and had previously commanded a torpedo boat. He stayed in the Royal Navy after the war, although dogged with negative evaluations; he went on half pay and then retired in 1929 as a lieutenant-commander.

Back in the 4th Flotilla, *Ambuscade* was mainly employed on convoy escort duties. This included anti-submarine work, and on 14 May 1918, she was involved in attacking a German U-boat with depth charges in Plymouth Sound, to no apparent result. The ship's log gives an indication of the procedure for searching, listening and then depth-charging an enemy submarine.

Ambuscade's final commander was Humphrey Jacomb. He was commissioned lieutenant in 1912 and commanded a patrol boat and a destroyer before joining *Ambuscade* in June 1918. He had a successful interwar career in the Royal Navy, being promoted to captain. He commanded the battleships HMS *Royal Sovereign* and HMS *Nelson* during the Second World War and finished his career as captain of HMS *Victory* and Commodore-in-Command Royal Navy Barracks, Portsmouth.

In August 1918, *Ambuscade* moved to the Northern Patrol Force based in Dundee. The ship's log records patrols along the east coast of Scotland and convoy escort duties, but no sign of enemy ships at the final stages of the war. On Armistice Day (11 November 1918) the crew were painting the ship in Kirkcaldy Bay.[29] Many ships were placed in reserve after the

---

[29]TNA, Ambuscade Ship's Log May-December 1918, ADM 53/33543

war ended in November 1918. *Ambuscade* was reduced to reserve at Devonport in June 1919. She was sold for scrap on 6 September 1921.

Conclusion

Royal Navy destroyers like *Ambuscade* had an active war. The unrealistic expectations of torpedo attacks on capital ships may not have been realised, but destroyers did play a crucial role. They protected the fleet, inhibited enemy trade and protected the convoys that supplied the British Isles and the Empire, developing a new role in anti-submarine warfare. They were the versatile successors to the frigates' role in the previous two centuries. Britain had 240 destroyers at the outbreak of war and built a further 294 by 1918. The Royal Navy lost 70 destroyers, the largest number (22) to mines, during the war. Destroyers also brought a new ethos to the Royal Navy. There was no room for the formality and class divisions which generally prevailed in the battle fleet. Often, very young officers had to make independent tactical decisions without waiting to be told what to do. That experience would be invaluable to the officers who went on to command the Royal Navy in the Second World War.

CHAPTER FOUR:
THE SECOND WORLD WAR

The Royal Navy emerged from the First World War with the largest fleet in the world, constituting half of the warships deployed by the world's big five remaining navies. However, the 1920s and 1930s' economic conditions resulted in savage cuts to defence spending and the Naval Estimates in particular. Somewhat ironically, this included Winston Churchill's time as chancellor of the Exchequer in 1925-26. UK governments operated a ten-year rule from 1919 until 1933, which assumed that the British Empire would not have to engage in a major war for ten years. This was also the period when disarmament was being pursued by all the major powers, with the Washington Treaty limiting the size of ships and navies. The hope was that the League of Nations (a forerunner of the United Nations) would resolve disputes by negotiation. The London Naval Conference of 1930 placed further limitations on the size of navies. In Britain's case, destroyer quotas were limited to 150,000 tons. Pay cuts for sailors in the Royal Navy in 1931 resulted in the Invergordon Mutiny (15-16 September 1931), one of the few military strikes in British history. The pay cuts were partially restored, but spending and the naval workforce were reduced further.

By the mid-1930s, a series of events, including the Abyssinian War, the Rome-Berlin Axis, and Japan's invasion of China, forced governments to rearm. From 1936 to 37, the Naval Estimates started to increase to fund a significant building programme, although never large enough or quickly enough, to face the prospect of a war with Japan, Germany and Italy simultaneously. When Germany invaded Poland in 1939, and

Britain declared war, the completed ships of the navies of the British Empire included 184 destroyers to carry out a wide range of roles across the globe. Royal Navy ships had limited air cover due to spending restrictions on the Fleet Air Arm, and shipborne antiaircraft defences proved inadequate. The U-boat threat to Britain's supply lines would be even more significant in the Second World War, and destroyers and other escort vessels would be required to protect the vital convoys. Smaller ships like destroyers were prioritised in wartime building programmes, which had the advantage of accessing US and Canadian shipyards. They would be needed, as British Empire navies lost 149 destroyers during the war.

The role of the destroyer was also changing. The fleet destroyers of the First World War had been designed to attack enemy warships, but now they served a more defensive role, protecting the fleet and escorting merchant convoys. While the main armament was similar, antiaircraft guns were now necessary to combat the new threat to ships from the air. Destroyers also had improved anti-submarine detection with the Asdic system introduced in 1922, which could detect a submarine at 2,500 yards (2,286m). The Royal Navy pioneered Radio Direction Finding (RDF) in 1938, better known by the later American term 'radar'. It could spot aircraft sixty nautical miles away, and later surface ships, initially ten miles away. These systems were developed during the war to detect ships and aircraft at a more extended range and for gunnery direction. Destroyers remained uncomfortable ships to serve in, particularly during wartime when crew size was increased to typically 125 officers and men. Messdecks were overcrowded, with inadequate heating and ventilation.

HMS *Ambuscade*

HMS *Ambuscade* was one of two prototype fleet destroyers ordered to an Admiralty specification to determine the design of the first new destroyers to be ordered for the Royal Navy after the end of WWI. They were to be armed as the war-built W-Class destroyers, but with a longer range of at least 5,000 nautical miles (9,300 km; 5,800 miles) at cruising speed. A speed of at least 34 knots (63 km/h; 39 mph) was required, and the ships were to be no more than 315 feet (96.01 m) long.

Tenders were invited from British shipbuilders who specialised in constructing this type of warship, and the winning bids came from Yarrow and Thorneycroft shipbuilders. *Ambuscade* was built at Yarrows, Glasgow. She was ordered on 12 June 1924, launched on 15 January 1926 and finally commissioned with the pennant number D38 on 9 April 1927. She was smaller and lighter than her Thorneycroft sister ship, *Amazon,* at 307 feet (93.57 m) long and 1,585 long tons (1,610 t) full load displacement. Her beam was 31 feet (9.45 m), with a draught of 8 feet, 6 inches (2.59 m).

HMS Ambuscade in coastal waters (Royal Navy official photographer, Public domain)

The main armament of *Ambuscade* consisted of four 4.7-inch breech-loading Mk I guns. These guns fired at a rate of about 5–6 rounds per gun per minute, with 190 shells carried per gun. Antiaircraft armament consisted of two 2-pdr pom-poms (with 100 rounds per gun) and four Lewis guns. The torpedo armament consisted of six 21-inch torpedo tubes in two triple mounts. During the Second World War, a 3-inch (76 mm) antiaircraft gun replaced the aft triple torpedo-tube mount. Two Oerlikon 20 mm cannons were added, and two 4.7-inch guns were removed. The ship's rangefinder and director were replaced with radar, and the Hedgehog anti-submarine mortar and a heavier depth charge outfit were installed. The ship's Hedgehog mount and remaining torpedo tubes were removed when the ship was fitted with two Squid launchers in May 1943. These improvements reflected the wartime development of warship design with heavier, quick-firing guns, more antiaircraft guns, and better anti-submarine weapons. Finally, workable radar systems were installed to detect ships and aircraft and to direct gunnery.

After commissioning, *Ambuscade* joined the Atlantic Fleet and cruised South America and the West Indies in 1928, with *Amazon*, to test the ship in tropical conditions, commanded by Commander A. T. N. Abbay DSO. This also involved 'flying the flag' in ports, which included sporting and social events, as well as showing off the latest in British warship design to potential customers. *Ambuscade* visited the Falkland Islands in June 1928, and the governor proudly reported that the colonial staff won the shooting, rowing, golf and billiards competitions, while the crew triumphed at football and boxing.[30] During the cruise, *Ambuscade* developed high temperatures in the engine room, suffered from vibration and had a shorter range than specified.[31] The commander and crew were

---

[30]TNA, Telegram from the Governor of the Falkland Islands, (9 June 1928), ADM 116/2618
[31]TNA, HMS Ambuscade reports of South American cruise 1928, ADM 116/2618

much impressed by the installation of a refrigerator in the ship and recommended their wider use in Royal Navy ships.

Local newspaper coverage of the visit to Buenos Aires

Commander L. H. K. Hamilton took command of *Ambuscade* in September 1928. He kept a journal that gives a flavour of life in the peacetime navy. It wasn't all refitting, training and 'showing the flag'. His journal includes the social events naval officers were expected to attend, sporting competitions including polo (he owned four ponies), and sailing regattas.[32]

In 1929, *Ambuscade* joined the Mediterranean Fleet but was hit by a practice torpedo and later developed turbine problems. These required repairs at Malta until 1931, when she returned to the UK and was placed in reserve. In 1932, she was back in service with the Home Fleet, supporting training and trials at the torpedo school. Further turbine problems resulted in a refit at Portsmouth, which continued until May 1940.

War Service

Following her refit in May 1940, *Ambuscade* joined the 16th Destroyer Flotilla based at Harwich, receiving a new pennant number, I38.

---

[32] L.Hamilton, Journal of HMS WILD SWAN on the China Station and commissioning HMS AMBUSCADE from Sheerness, the Mediterranean and Portsmouth 1928/29, (National Maritime Museum, Greenwich).

The Germans invaded France in May 1940, and the Blitzkrieg campaign quickly knocked France out of the war, forcing the evacuation of the British Expeditionary Force (BEF) from Dunkirk. The 51st (Highland) Division was detached from the BEF serving with the French Third Army defending the Maginot Line. It suffered heavy casualties in the German attack and retreated westwards with the French forces. Cut off from the BEF, they reached the coast at Saint-Valery-en-Caux, blocked by German troops from reaching the planned evacuation from Le Havre. On 10 June, *Ambuscade* took part in the attempt to evacuate the troops from Saint-Valery-en-Caux as part of Operation Cycle. With steep cliffs overlooking the small harbour, the Germans could pour fire onto the evacuation, and *Ambuscade* was damaged by German shell fire while embarking troops. On the journey back to Portsmouth, she took the destroyer HMS *Boadicea* in tow after German dive bombers severely damaged the latter. More than ten thousand members of the 51st (Highland) Infantry Division were taken prisoner at St Valery.

Saint-Valery-en-Caux today showing how the cliffs dominate the beach

Ambuscade rejoined her flotilla after repairs, carrying out anti-invasion patrols and convoy escort duties in July and August 1940. She transferred to the 12th Destroyer Flotilla based at Greenock in September 1940, but the recurrence of the ship's turbine problems resulted in more repairs from September to November 1940.

After these repairs, *Ambuscade* was based in Iceland for convoy escort duties. Iceland was in personal union through King Christian X of

Denmark, and declared neutrality after the Germans occupied Denmark in April 1940. The British invaded Iceland on 10 May 1940 (Operation Fork) because the British feared that it would be used as a military base by Germany. On 7 July 1941, the defence of Iceland was transferred from Britain to the United States. Reykjavik was used as a staging point for convoys, although it could be attacked by U-boats and German Fw 200 Kondor maritime patrol aircraft based in Norway.

Air and submarine attacks could be made on convoys en route to Iceland, and fighter air cover was not always available. Convoy reports by *Ambuscade* highlighted a range of challenges including bad weather, slow merchant ships (seven knots was considered the minimum necessary in winter) and bad coal that smoked too much.[33] *Ambuscade* could spot the convoy smoke some fifteen miles away, which the CinC Western Approaches described as 'deplorable'. By 1941 convoys were getting better at station keeping and keeping their ship darkened. Further mechanical problems, this time with the ship's condensers, forced more repairs at Portsmouth between October 1941 and January 1942.

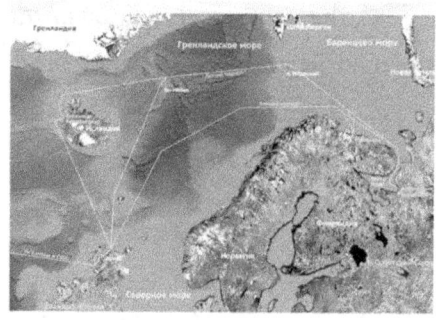

Soviet map showing the convoy routes (Mil.ru, CC BY 4.0)

In March 1942, *Ambuscade* formed part of the Arctic convoy PQ 14 on its leg from Scotland to Iceland. Arctic convoys were dispatched to the Soviet Union with lend-lease equipment and other supplies to the Soviet ports in northern Russia. In October 1941, Prime Minister Winston Churchill committed to send a convoy to the Arctic ports of the USSR

---

[33]TNA, HMS Ambuscade on convoys OB 275 and HX 101, (25 Jan. 1941), ADM 199/1141

every ten days. This was not without challenges. The Arctic Ocean includes some of the stormiest waters of the world's oceans, with gales full of snow, sleet, and hail. Around the North Cape and the Barents Sea, the sea temperature rarely rises above 4° Celsius, and a man falling overboard would die unless rescued immediately. The cold water and air made spray freeze on the superstructure of ships, which had to be removed quickly to avoid the ship becoming top-heavy. Despite the weather, winter convoys were less hazardous because the short days limited air attacks by the Luftwaffe.

As Germany's invasion of the Soviet Union reached a crucial stage in March 1942, Hitler ordered the German navy and air force to step up attacks on convoys from their bases in northern Norway. Luftflotte 5 (air fleet) was reinforced with more long-range Focke-Wulf Fw 200 Kondor patrol aircraft and dive-bombers, totalling 221 frontline planes. The reconnaissance aircraft would spot and follow convoys, directing attacks by dive-bombers, German Kriegsmarine ships, and U-boats.

Convoy PQ 14 included six British, ten US, two Soviet, one Dutch and one Panamanian-flagged merchant ships. They gathered at Oban and sailed for Iceland on 26 March 1942 with the destroyer escorts *Ambuscade*, *Błyskawica* (Polish),[34] HMS *Bulldog* and HMS *Richmond*. Convoys had a standard formation of short columns, sailing at intervals of 400 yards (370 m). There was also a distant escort of heavier warships, including the battleships HMS *Duke of York* and *King George V*, the aircraft carrier HMS *Victorious*, together with five cruisers and fourteen destroyers. *Ambuscade's* sister ship, *Amazon*, joined the convoy escort after Iceland. The journey to Iceland was uneventful, and *Ambuscade* completed its escort role. Between Iceland and its destination, Murmansk, the convoy

---

[34] You can visit Błyskawica in Gdynia, Poland today, https://muzeummw.pl/en/orp-blyskawica-a-real-war-veteran/

was spotted on 15 April by the Luftwaffe and was attacked by aircraft, submarines and surface ships. Fog and pack ice caused so much damage that sixteen vessels had to turn back and return to Iceland, one merchant ship was sunk, and the seven remaining ships in the convoy reached Murmansk. The fog probably saved the remaining ships, as the convoy heard the German aircraft above the low cloud searching for them.

Junkers Ju 88 D-2, in Kirkenes, Norway (Der Adler (Zeitschrift), Public domain)

Some nineteen merchant ships made up the return convoy QP 9, mainly carrying timber. Returning convoys had no military supplies, making them a lower attack priority for the Germans. However, U-boats attacked the convoy, and one (*U-655*) was rammed and sunk by the minesweeper HMS *Sharpshooter*. *Ambuscade* formed part of the escort back from Iceland. By this time, it was clear that *Ambuscade's* reoccurring mechanical problems meant that the ship was not fit for convoy escort duties, and she was assigned target duties. These typically involved the ship towing targets for naval gunnery practice or weapons testing.

While some convoys, most notably PQ 17, were badly mauled, the convoy system was successful. As Admiral of the Fleet Lord Lewin, who served in convoy escorts, puts it, 'In fact, the Arctic convoys were amazingly successful. Of a total of 40 outward convoys comprising 811 ships, only 58 were sunk. Those that got through delivered great quantities of tanks, aircraft, ammunition and other essential war material which made a significant contribution to Russia's role in the war'.[35]

In late 1942, *Ambuscade* became a trials ship for anti-submarine weapons and sensors, being fitted with the experimental 'Parsnip' anti-submarine mortar in an attempt to provide a more capable anti-submarine weapon than 'Hedgehog'. 'Parsnip' was not a success, and in May 1943, *Ambuscade* was fitted with the prototype installation of the 'Squid' anti-submarine mortar and its associated depth-finding Type 147 sonar. This sonar would typically pick up the U-boat at about eight hundred yards and automatically put the correct setting on the Squid projectiles. Trials of Squid were successful, and the weapon was widely fitted in new construction Royal Navy escorts. *Ambuscade* continued as a trial and training platform until the end of the war in Europe, and then she went into reserve.

Ambuscade was used for shock trials during 1946 and was sold for scrapping in November of that year, being broken up by West of Scotland Shipbreaking Company at Troon in March 1947.

The *Ambuscade* design was the basis for the *Douro*-class destroyers, which served in the Portuguese Navy from 1933 to 1967. Five vessels were ordered by Portugal in 1932. The first two were sold to the Colombian Navy before their 1933 completion. This was in response to the Colombia–Peru War, and they served the Colombians as the *Antioquia* class. The Portuguese Navy ordered two further ships to replace them. Two of the ships were built at Yarrow's shipyard in

---

[35]R. Woodman, Arctic Convoys, 1941–1945, (Pen & Sword Books, 2018), p. 13

Clydebank, and the remainder were built in Lisbon with Yarrow machinery. Despite these foreign orders, it has to be conceded that the *Ambuscade* design was not a success. This is often the case for prototype designs used to test new concepts.

Douro-class destroyer Lima (Yarrow, Public domain)

Merchant Navy

As we have seen, a key role for *Ambuscade* and other destroyers was convoy escort duty. Their exploits are remembered in film and books such as the classic 1953 war film *The Cruel Sea*, starring Jack Hawkins, with its famous voice-over:

'This is a story of the Battle of the Atlantic, the story of an ocean, two ships, and a handful of men. The men are the heroes; the heroines are the ships. The only villain is the sea, the cruel sea, that man has made more cruel.'

Often overlooked in this narrative is the role of the Merchant Navy.

During the Second World War, the Merchant Navy was vital in supplying Britain and its allies with essential goods, including food, fuel, and weapons. Despite facing significant dangers from enemy submarines, mines, and surface raiders, merchant ships continued transporting goods across the Atlantic and other war zones. The Battle of the Atlantic, which lasted throughout the war, saw intense efforts by German U-boats to sink Allied shipping convoys. Still, the merchant marine, along with naval escorts and technological innovations such as sonar and convoy tactics, ultimately helped to defeat the U-boat threat.

Wartime poster highlighting the dangers the Merchant Navy faced.

Merchant seamen faced tremendous risks, with thousands losing their lives due to enemy action or accidents at sea. Around 27 per cent of all serving British merchant seafarers in WW2 died, a much higher proportion than those serving in the armed forces. Between May 1940 and May 1944, 2,284 British merchant ships were sunk, along with 1,635 Allied merchant ships and 317 from neutral countries.

The 185,000 merchant seaman serving in the Merchant Navy came from all over the world, and their service has only recently been recognised. A 1938 survey found that 27 per cent were from India or China, and another five per cent were British-domiciled Arabs, Indians, Chinese, West Africans or West Indians, mainly residents in major UK ports. Their contributions were crucial in sustaining the Allied war effort and ensuring the survival of Britain and its allies. Not that many got any thanks. In December 1945 and throughout 1946, the police and immigration inspectorate in Liverpool began the process of forcibly rounding up some 20,000 Chinese seamen, putting them on boats and sending them to an uncertain future in China. Many deported Chinese seamen had met and married English women, had children and settled in Liverpool. The families were never told what was happening, never given a chance to object and never allowed to say goodbye.

Aid to the Soviet Union was a political challenge for a fervent anti-communist like Winston Churchill. He managed to sell his new line of supporting the Soviets with classic Churchillian rhetoric, 'If Hitler invaded hell, I would make at least a favourable reference to the devil in the House of Commons.' However, playing *The Internationale* with other Allied anthems on the BBC was a step too far for Churchill! The Communist Party of Great Britain's (CPGB) *Daily Worker* newspaper remained banned until August 1942. Churchill's wife Clementine was the driving force behind raising funds for Russia, so much so that Churchill told the Soviet ambassador that his wife had become 'totally sovietised'. The CPGB may not have made much progress politically. Still, they were particularly well organised in the trade unions representing industrial workers on the Clyde and elsewhere and achieved significant victories for workers on the home front.[36]

---

[36] C. Turbett, The Anglo-Soviet Alliance: Comrades and Allies during WW2, (Pen & Sword, 2021)

The Clyde shipyards didn't only build warships like *Ambuscade*. The River Clyde and Glasgow were pivotal in WW2, providing a seaport safer from the Luftwaffe than those further south. Five hundred million tons of shipping moved into and out of Glasgow, bringing cargo and troops from the USA. The Clyde shipyards also built 1,903 naval and merchant ships and converted a further 637 for wartime uses. Many naval and air bases were established along the coast to protect the Clyde during wartime. These included a boom defence at the entrance to the Clyde near Gourock, consisting of a steel net defended by boom defence vessels and shore batteries.[37]

On 30 October 1945, the House of Commons paid the following tribute to the Merchant Navy:

'That the thanks of this House be accorded to the officers and men of the Merchant Navy for the steadfastness with which they maintained our stocks of food and materials; for their services in transporting men and munitions to all the battles over all the seas; and for the gallantry with which, though a civilian service, they met and fought the constant attacks of the enemy.'

---

[37] C. Turbett, Witness to War: Arran and the Firth of Clyde in the Second World War, (AANHS, 2023)

CHAPTER FIVE:
TODAY'S HMS *AMBUSCADE*

Type 21 Frigates

In 1966, the government decided to phase out the Royal Navy's aircraft carriers, and with that decision went most of the planned Type 82 destroyer escorts. A smaller type of warship was in development with the Type 42 destroyer and Type 22 frigate. However, this left insufficient modern fleet escorts for the Royal Navy's needs. The Royal Navy was also concerned about the dramatic growth in Soviet naval strength, which was deploying increasing numbers and types of anti-ship missiles. New frigates were expected to provide a high degree of protection to their parent ships and to be able to operate independently. All of this is in the context of tight budgets and increasing shipbuilding costs.[38]

Commercial tenders were invited because the Royal Navy's design department was busy with the new warships. The contract for a new warship class, designated Type 21 (*Amazon* class), was awarded to Vosper Thornycroft in February 1968. Yarrow Shipbuilders on the Clyde was nominated to assist with the design and the building programme. This design would provide a 'stopgap replacement' for *Leander*-class frigates and enable the companies 'to sell to other navies with the cachet that it had been ordered for the RN'.[39] HMS *Ambuscade* was laid down at Yarrow's on 1 September 1971 as part of a class of eight ships: *Amazon*,

---

[38]TNA, Type 22 Frigate, MoD Operational Requirements Committee, (Feb. 1972) T225/4274.
[39]TNA, Type 21, MoD Director of Resources and Programmes, (Dec. 73), T225/4274.

Antelope, Active, Ambuscade, Arrow, Alacrity, Ardent and *Avenger*. They were completed between 1974 and 1978. *Ambuscade* was the first of the five Yarrow-built ships, launched on 18 January 1973 by Lady Griffin, completed on 5 May 1975 and commissioned at Devonport on 5 September 1975. She carried the pennant number F172. There was a significant increase in cost from the original estimates. However, the MoD and the Treasury accepted that the reasons were outside Yarrow's control.

The streamlined modern design with a sharply raked bow won many plaudits. Their new technical feature was that they were the first major warships designed to be entirely propelled by gas turbines. Two Rolls-Royce Olympus gas turbines produced a maximum speed of 32 knots (59 km/h; 37 mph) at full load. For cruising, two Rolls-Royce Tyne engines produced a speed of 18 knots. This gave the ship exceptional flexibility, and if damaged in combat, the ship could run on one shaft driven by either of the engines. The engine exhausts were trunked through a broad, squat funnel, which gave the ship its distinctive appearance.

Ambuscade was designed as a general-purpose frigate and consequently carried a mixed armament. The main gun was a new design for a frigate, the 4.5-inch (114 mm) Mark 8 naval gun. This had been adapted for shipboard use from the British Army's Abbot self-propelled gun. It featured an automatic-loading system that could fire 25 rounds per minute, and a holding magazine of 15 rounds could be fired without the turret being crewed. After that, the magazines had to be replaced manually. This gun had a maximum range of 14 miles (22 km). The only other guns were two single 20mm Oerlikon cannons mounted on either side of the bridge.

Ambuscade alongside the Devonport Frigate Complex in November 1985 (Leo Marriott/ Air Sea Media)

For anti-aircraft defence, a quadruple Seacat missile launcher was mounted on the roof of the helicopter hanger towards the stern (rear) of the ship. Seacat was a British short-range surface-to-air missile system designed by Short Brothers of Belfast. It was first introduced in 1962 and was intended to replace the ubiquitous Bofors 40mm gun aboard warships of all sizes. It was the world's first operational shipboard point-defence missile system, although it was probably obsolete by the 1970s due to higher aircraft speeds. However, it was still in service during the Falklands War in 1982, proving more reliable than its replacement, the Sea Wolf missile. *Ambuscade* also had a pair of 8-barrelled, 3-inch chaff dispensers fitted forward of the bridge for electronic countermeasure (ECM) purposes. This system dispersed thin strips of metallised glass fibre, producing an echo with a large radar cross section intended to distract missiles guided by active radar homing, causing them to miss the ship.

For anti-submarine warfare (ASW) work, the ship had a landing pad and hanger, initially for a Westland Wasp helicopter. The ship carried sonars (Type 184M and Type 162M) to detect submarines, which the helicopter would then attack with a torpedo. The advantage compared to traditional shipboard weapons was that submarines could be attacked well away from the ship. The Wasp had a crew of two (pilot and missile aimer/aircrewman) and the capacity to seat three passengers. It was useful for short-range transport missions and casualty evacuation, with room for one stretcher fitted across the rear cabin area. The Westland Lynx helicopter quickly replaced the Wasp, which could carry a heavier weapon load over a longer distance. Weapons included Sting Ray torpedoes, Sea Skua anti-ship missiles and depth charges.

Royal Navy Lynx (heb@Wikimedia Commons (mail), CC BY-SA 2.5

One of the significant design advances was the provision of advanced electronics to help run the ship. The Computer Assisted Action Information System (CAAIS) was operated from six consoles in the operations room. This system could be programmed to assist in target selection and recommend the best weapon to use. The introduction of advanced electronics meant the ship's complement of 177 crew was significantly smaller than the 250 or more in other frigates, smaller than the Type 21. These electronic systems were updated during the ship's service.

There was some initial criticism that the Type 21 frigates were under-armed in relation to their size and cost. This led to introducing the French Exocet anti-ship missile, installed in four canister launchers mounted in pairs forward of the bridge. The Exocet is a guided missile using active radar homing late in its flight to find and hit its target. It maintains a very low altitude while inbound, skimming just a few feet above the waves. The effect of the radar horizon means that the target may not detect an incoming attack until the missile is only about four miles from impact, leaving little time for reaction. The plan was to install this system on all Type 21 frigates. However, *Ambuscade* did not receive hers until 1984-85, after the Falklands War. While helicopter ASW provision had advantages over shipboard weapons, it was decided to add the shipboard Plessey STWS-1 ASW torpedo system, which gave the crew an immediate defence capability close to the ship and when the helicopter was not available.

HMS *Ambuscade*

Like all new ships, *Ambuscade* conducted a series of sea trials, under her first captain Commander Anthony Harris, before joining Standing Naval Force Atlantic (STANAVFORLANT), one of NATO's maritime immediate reaction forces. The Type 21 frigate, including HMS *Ambuscade,* was well received by its crews. It had a good standard of crew accommodation, and its rakish style engendered a feeling of pride in the ship—often referred to as the 'Porsche' or 'greyhound' of the fleet.

The next captain was Commander Peter Abbot, who joined the ship in 1976.[40] During his command, the ship performed regular peacetime duties, including training, visits and security patrols. In September 1976, *Ambuscade* took part in Exercise Northern Wedding as an escort for the aircraft carrier *Ark Royal* in the Norwegian Sea.

In 1978, *Ambuscade* (Commander Michael Gretton)[41] joined the 5th Frigate Squadron, operating in the Western Atlantic and the Pacific, before returning to home waters in 1979. Later, in 1979, she deployed to Belize and served as the guard ship in the West Indies before returning to Devonport for home duties and a refit in 1980. (A guard ship is a warship allocated to a port or region for immediate defence purposes.)

In late 1980, *Ambuscade* (Commander Bryan Burns), with *Active* and *Ardent*, was deployed to the Persian Gulf (Armilla Patrol) to protect British and international shipping during the Iran-Iraq War. Iraq under Saddam Hussein had invaded Iran in September 1980.[42] *Ambuscade*, now captained by Commander Peter Mosse, was returning home from the Armilla Patrol deployment through the Red Sea in February 1982 when she went to the assistance of the tanker MV *Aris*, which had caught fire. A firefighting team went aboard for around twenty-four hours, helping to bring the fire under control.

The Falklands War 1982

The Falkland Islands (Islas Malvinas) are about 300 miles (480 km) off the coast of Argentina. The 3,662 inhabitants are primarily native-

---

[40] Peter Abbot subsequently became Commander-in-Chief Fleet and, having been promoted to admiral in 1995, he became Vice-Chief of the Defence Staff in 1997.
[41] Michael Gretton at thirty-one years old was the youngest captain of a major surface warship. He retired as a vice-admiral.
[42] The conflict later developed into the so-called 'Tanker War' when Iraq attacked the oil terminal and oil tankers at Kharg Island in early 1984. The aim was to provoke the Iranians to retaliate by closing the Strait of Hormuz to all maritime traffic, thereby bringing international intervention.

born Falkland Islanders, mostly of British descent. The islands have had French, British, Spanish, and Argentine settlements at various times. Britain reasserted its rule in 1833, but Argentina maintained its claim to the islands.

In 1965, the United Nations called upon Argentina and the United Kingdom to settle the sovereignty dispute. The UK Foreign and Commonwealth Office (FCO) was prepared to cede the islands to Argentina in return for a trade agreement, as they had lost their strategic value. However, the islanders organised an influential parliamentary lobby to frustrate the FCO plans. Negotiations continued, including a proposed leaseback deal in 1980, but failed to make meaningful progress. The islanders refused to consider Argentine sovereignty on one side, whilst Argentina would not compromise over sovereignty on the other.

In early 1982, the unpopular military junta led by General Leopoldo Galtieri (acting president), Air Brigadier Basilio Lami Dozo and Admiral Jorge Anaya hoped to divert public attention from the chronic economic problems and the ongoing human rights violations of its Dirty War by invading the islands. Britain had sent mixed messages over its willingness to defend the islands, including publishing plans to withdraw the icebreaker HMS *Endurance*, the UK's only naval presence in the South Atlantic.

On 2 April 1982, Argentinian forces launched amphibious landings (Operation Rosario) backed up by commandos, a marine battalion, and armoured vehicles. The British garrison consisted of sixty-eight Royal Marines, twenty-three Falkland Islands Defence Force volunteers, and eleven naval hydrographers. This force resisted fiercely, killing one Argentinian marine and wounding six more (precise casualties are contested). However, when the armoured vehicles arrived at Government House, Governor Rex Hunt recognised that his forces had nothing to counter them and ordered the troops to surrender. On 3 April 1982, the United Nations Security Council passed Resolution 502, demanding an immediate withdrawal of all Argentine forces from the islands and calling on both governments to seek a diplomatic solution and refrain from further military action. An emergency meeting of the UK cabinet approved forming a task force to retake the islands (Operation Corporate), which was backed in an emergency sitting of the House of Commons the next day.

The initial Argentinian garrison was the 25th Infantry Regiment (681 men). However, when it was clear that the UK was sending a task force, the garrison was strengthened with conscripts and reserves from eight regiments, numbering around 13,000 troops. The Argentinian Air Force had 122 serviceable jet fighters, of which about 50 were used as air superiority fighters and the remainder as strike aircraft. The Argentinian Navy deployed in three task groups. The first included the aircraft carrier *Veinticinco de Mayo* with two old but missile-armed destroyers. The second comprised three modern frigates, all approaching from the north. A third group approaching from the south was led by the light cruiser *General Belgrano*, which, although old, had large guns and heavy armour, and she was escorted by two modern British-built Type 42 guided-missile destroyers armed with Exocet missiles.

The British task force eventually comprised 127 ships: 43 Royal Navy vessels, 22 Royal Fleet Auxiliary ships, and 62 merchant ships. It included all of the Royal Navy's Type 21 frigates, except *Amazon*, as part of the Fourth Frigate Squadron (Captain White). Air cover would be provided by two aircraft carriers, HMS *Invincible* and HMS *Hermes*, with 28 Sea Harriers supplemented by 14 Royal Air Force (RAF) Harrier GR.3s. The Carrier/Battle Group commander was Rear Admiral J.F. (Sandy) Woodward. An air base defended by Phantom fighters was established on Ascension Island, which provided a base for Avro Vulcan bombers and refuelling tankers. The Vulcans attacked the airfield at Stanley (Operation Black Buck). The attack did minor damage, but it forced the Argentinian Air Force to deploy its fast jets on the mainland.

Advanced Group leaving Gibraltar (Pete Reeves, CC BY 4.0)

The British island of South Georgia lies around 870 miles (1400 km) east of the Falkland Islands. It had an intermittent population, and on 19 March, a group of Argentinians landed, followed by naval forces after 2 April. A Royal Navy force was tasked with its recapture (Operation Paraquet), including SAS and SBS troops and marines from 42 Commando. The submarine HMS *Conqueror* arrived on 19 April, and the RAF flew observation flights. The Argentinian Navy attempted to resupply their troops by submarine on 25 April. However, the *Santa Fe* was attacked by several helicopters from Royal Navy warships, and the crew abandoned the submarine at a jetty, augmenting the garrison to around 190 troops. The British commander decided to assault the position with a force of 76 men supported by gunfire from HMS *Antrim* and HMS *Plymouth*. The Argentinian forces surrendered without resistance.

Back in the Falkland Islands, the British had imposed a Total Exclusion Zone (TEZ), covering a radius of 200 miles around the islands. Five Royal Navy submarines were deployed off the Argentinian coast to provide early warning of attacks on the task force, which arrived on 29 April. The Argentinian cruiser *General Belgrano* was spotted on the edge of the TEZ on 2 May and was sunk by two torpedoes from the submarine HMS *Conqueror*, causing 321 crew to lose their lives, while a further 700 were rescued. The controversial attack forced the Argentinian fleet back to base, and the fleet took no further part in the conflict.

The Argentinian Air Force was able to resupply the garrison at night and made several attacks on ships of the task force. On 4 May, HMS *Sheffield* (Type 42 Destroyer) was hit by a missile, killing twenty crew members. She sank six days later, the first Royal Navy ship sunk in action since the Second World War.

On 21 May, *Ardent* (one of *Ambuscade*'s Yarrow-built sister ships) was sunk. She was bombarding Goose Green in support of the land battle when she was caught in the open waters of the Falkland Sound by Argentinian aircraft and was hit by nine bombs. The ship caught fire and sank, with twenty-two crew killed and a further thirty injured. A bomb hit another Type 21 frigate, HMS *Antelope*, on 23 May. It failed to explode, but was later detonated after a failed attempt to defuse it, and *Antelope* sank in San Carlos waters. On 25 May, the Type 42 destroyer HMS *Coventry* was sunk by bombs in Falkland Sound. Casualties and ship losses could have been higher, but the low altitude release of bombs meant many fuses had insufficient time to arm.

The land battle started on 21 May with amphibious landings in San Carlos. By dawn the next day a bridgehead had been secured by 3 Commando Brigade. 2 Para with fire support from *Arrow* captured Goose

Green on 28 May. During this attack, Lieutenant Colonel H. Jones was killed at the head of his battalion while charging into the Argentine positions. He was posthumously awarded the Victoria Cross.

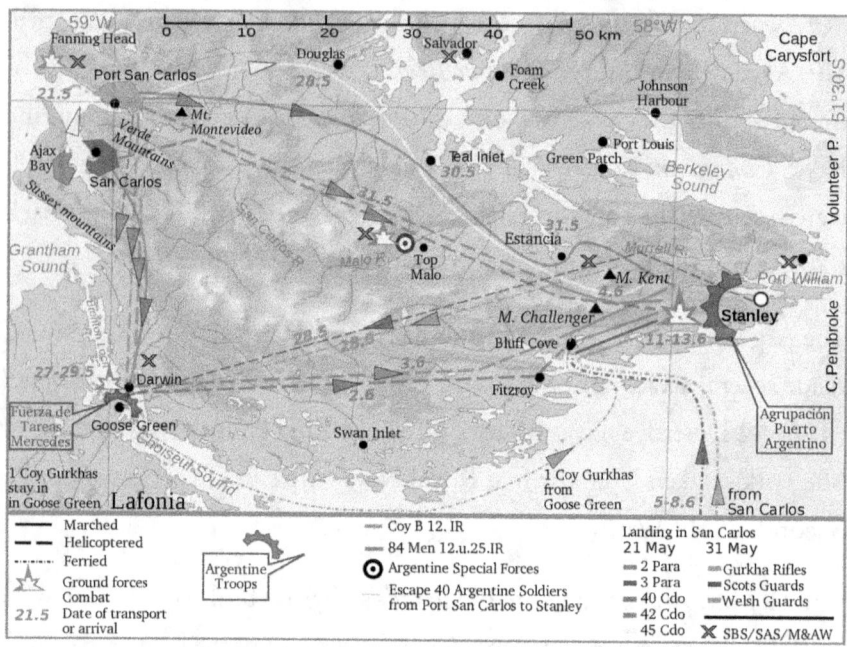

Falklands War – land operations (Falkland_Islands_topographic_map-en.svg: Eric Gaba (Sting - fr:Sting)derivative work: Createaccount, GFDL)

Meanwhile, *Ambuscade* (Cdr Peter Mosse)[43] had sailed from Plymouth on 9 April en route to Gibraltar with a resupply of ammunition for the garrison. As the flight deck was used for ammunition storage, there was no opportunity to undertake flight operations on the passage to Gibraltar, and further repairs were necessary at the Gibraltar airfield (RAF Northfront).[44]

---

[43] After Ambuscade, Peter Mosse served on the British Navy Staff in Washington DC and then in the MOD on future Electronic Warfare (EW) requirements. He retired in 2001, working in facilities management and supporting veterans charities establishing drop-in centres. He also serves on the Clyde Naval Heritage Advisory Group.

[44] P. Mosse, HMS Ambuscade – Flight report of proceedings Operation Corporate, (TNA, 24 July 1982, DEFE 69/817).

Ambuscade was then to take over as the Gibraltar guard ship for three weeks before returning to the UK. However, after the Argentine invasion, she was ordered to sail for Ascension Island to serve as the guard ship there, arriving on 10 May. On 13 May, she was ordered to join the task force in company with *Antelope,* which had arrived with Argentinian prisoners from South Georgia.

Two days out from Ascension, one of the ship's Tyne engines broke down. This created a fuel problem, as maintaining a speed of 18 knots using the Olympus engine would reduce the fuel to below safety limits. It was decided to slow to 14 knots using the good Tyne engine while *Antelope* went on ahead. They met the tanker with 28 per cent fuel left, one per cent below what was needed for the ship's stability. This was just enough because of all the extra stores carried low down in the ship, but it was a close thing. However, a Force 10 gale created further problems and the tanker's fuel hoses couldn't get enough pressure. This brought the fuel level down to 20 per cent and risk of capsizing, so the fuel tanks had to be ballasted with sea water. Unbeknown to the captain, the stokers volunteered to go down into tanks and scrub them out with soap and water so they could be used again, a most unpleasant job, especially in rough seas. They knew that if the ship had clean tanks in time they could then fill her right up again from the next tanker, which is what happened.

Ambuscade arrived in the TEZ on 22 May amid the air attacks and joined the Battle Group. On that day, *Ambuscade* had a minor collision with RFA *Tidepool* (*Tide*-class replenishment oiler) during the transfer of equipment, although without severe damage. *Ambuscade* was initially deployed as part of the ASW screen. On 23 May, a sonar contact showed a submarine heading for *Invincible*, and one crew member heard a torpedo. *Ambuscade* fired an anti-submarine torpedo.

On 25 May, *Ambuscade* detected two Argentinian Super Étendard aircraft to the north on her Electronic Warfare (EW) equipment, and then picked them up on radar as they climbed to fire their Exocet missiles, probably aimed at *Hermes*. Seeing missile separation from the aircraft on radar, *Ambuscade* signalled a warning, which enable *Hermes* to escape at full speed. Although they only saw one missile, *Ambuscade*'s crew successfully decoyed both missiles from hitting the ship using chaff from its 4.5-inch gun; but flying on, the missiles locked onto a larger target, the container ship SS *Atlantic Conveyor*. Both missiles hit the ship, and the subsequent fires could not be contained, destroying three Chinook and six Wessex helicopters allocated to support land operations. Twelve men died in *Atlantic Conveyor*, including the ship's master, Captain Ian North, who was posthumously awarded the Distinguished Service Cross (DSC). The ship was the first British merchant vessel lost at sea to enemy fire since the Second World War.

```
1800
1922  LYNX ONBOARD      SHUT DOWN         1940ctd  FIRED CHAFF 4.5 SEACAT
1936  AGAVE RADAR DETECTED                20MM AND S.A. FIRE ON STBD
1937  HANDS TO ACTION STATIONS            QUARTER. MISSILE OBSERVED TO
1938  RADAR LOCKED ON                     PASS ASTERN "ATLANTIC
1940  ACTION STATIONS CLOSED UP           CONVEYOR" HIT AFT
2009  Supor[elected] / 2exocet attack     1956  ALL HOSTILES OUT BOUND
                                          1 MISFIRED  4.5" ROUND DITCHED
2005  CLOSED ATLANTIC CONVEYOR
      TO ASSIST
2010  ABANDONING FROM "CONVEYOR"
2027  LIGHT SEEN IN WATER
2023  SEABOAT LAUNCHED
2058  SEABOAT RECOVERED - NO SURVIVORS RESCUED BY SEABOAT
2115  COMMENCE SEARCHLIGHT SEARCH
2150  REVERT TO DEFENCE WATCHES
2217  OPENED FROM BURNING "ATLANTIC CONVEYOR" TO 5NM
```

HMS Ambuscade ship's log records the action on 25 May 1982 and the sinking of the Atlantic Conveyor.

Having demonstrated her undoubted EW prowess, from now on when she was with the Task Group, *Ambuscade* was stationed as EW picket as part of the outer Air Defence screen with the Type 42 destroyers.

The successful landings and the action at Goose Green enabled an advance from San Carlos to Mount Kent, which overlooked Stanley. A supporting attack by the newly arrived 5th Infantry Brigade in Bluff Cove/Port Pleasant went badly wrong, leaving the Welsh Guards on board the landing ships RFA *Sir Tristram* and RFA *Sir Galahad*. Both were sitting ducks for an air attack that killed 48 and wounded 115 more. On the night of 11 June, a brigade-strength attack on the mountains around Stanley succeeded after fierce fighting, particularly on Mount Longdon. A second phase attack on 13 June led to the capture of the final Argentinian positions on Wireless Ridge and Mount Tumbledown. The commander of the Argentine garrison in Stanley, Brigade General Mario Menéndez, surrendered to Major General Jeremy Moore on 14 June. A total of 649 Argentine and 255 British service personnel were killed, with a further 1,188 Argentine and 777 British injured or wounded. Three civilians were accidentally killed by British shelling.

Ambuscade was heavily involved in supporting land operations, screening transports, and providing naval gunfire to Argentinian positions. She escorted convoys of transport ships to the islands at night because Argentinian aircraft had no night attack capabilities. Her Lynx helicopter inserted special forces onto the island from *Avenger*. Her crew fired on positions around Port Stanley on 30 May. In the first week of June, *Ambuscade* bombarded positions around the Teal Inlet and later Mount Harriet to the west of Port Stanley in support of the final assault. *Ambuscade* fired 228 shells in support of 2 Para's advance on Wireless Ridge above the town. The ship's 4.5-inch gun was computer-aided, and could store eight target positions and engage two of them at once. The accuracy of their fire meant 2 Para could take out enemy batteries just a few hundred yards ahead of them, and while they didn't kill many of the young conscripts, in the words of an Argentinian officer, 'They were stunned'.

```
0400
0405 ARRIVED ON GUNLINE
0410 ENGAGED FIRST TARGET 20 ROUNDS HE
0412 ENGAGED SECOND TARGET 15 ROUNDS HE
0445 ENGAGED THIRD TARGET  20 ROUNDS HE
0455 ENGAGED FOURTH TARGET 15 ROUNDS HE
0515 ENGAGED FIFTH TARGET 15 ROUNDS HE
0600 CEASED FIRE DEFECT IN TURRET
     START AND SELECT FIRE ON PROCEEDING TO RE Jopl TIME ACTIVE FINGER complete DUE TO TARGET
     DEFECT.
0720 THREE STARSHELL SIGHTED TWO RED 150° ONE RED 180°
0731 HANDS TO ACTION STATIONS RESUME NBCD STATE 1Z.
0755 SECURED FROM ACTION STATIONS
0800
```

This is a typical Ambuscade ship's log entry for 7 June, showing the scale of shore bombardment.

It wasn't one-way traffic. Shore batteries fired back at the ship, and there was a land-based Exocet battery to contend with. The Argentinians had also laid a minefield in the approaches to Port Stanley. As Commander Mosse commented afterwards, 'Although these kept us on our toes, I was more frightened of getting our propellers tangled up in the huge fields of kelp extensively marked on the chart.'[45]

After the surrender, *Ambuscade* undertook various duties supporting the land operations and maintaining the air defence screen. Finally, she entered Port Stanley harbour on 4 July and embarked 40 soldiers from the 2nd Battalion Scots Guards to relieve M Company Royal Marines in South Georgia. She arrived in South Georgia on 7 July, and after disembarking the Scots Guards and taking M Company RMs onboard, she sailed for Ascension Island and home. She arrived in Plymouth on 24 July for some well-deserved leave for the crew and repairs to the ship. *Ambuscade* had been at sea for 83 days, had steamed 29,226 nautical miles, fired 500 4.5-inch shells, and her helicopter had made 377 deck landings.[46]

The islanders had full British citizenship restored in 1983, and Argentina returned to a democratic government in the 1983 general election. The

---

[45] A. Wooley, Hopes are high for fast frigate that served two navies well to play a starring role on the Clyde, (Warships International Fleet Review, 2023).
[46] L. Marriot, Royal Navy Frigates 1945-1983, (Ian Allan, 1983), p. 104.

airfield and port facilities were rebuilt to create 'Fortress Falklands' with conventional RAF fighters and a garrison. The proposed defence cuts were quietly dropped. There is a memorial to the dead in Stanley and in the crypt of St Paul's Cathedral. A Falklands War memorial was unveiled at the National Memorial Arboretum in Staffordshire in May 2012. A study of British combat veterans found that half of the sample group had suffered some symptoms of post-traumatic stress disorder (PTSD) while 22 per cent were assessed to have the complete syndrome. Around ninety-five veterans committed suicide and open verdict deaths.

Diplomatic relations between the UK and Argentina were restored in 1989. Argentina adopted a new constitution in 2004, which declared the Falkland Islands as part of one of its provinces. However, the islands continue to operate as a self-governing British Overseas Territory.

There was some post-war criticism of the destroyers' aluminium superstructure design when subjected to intense heat, such as in the sinkings of *Antelope* and *Ardent*. However, while lessons should always be learned, others argued that no other contemporary warship would have taken similar damage and survived. Rear Admiral Woodward wrote to Captain White, commanding the Fourth Frigate Squadron, 'My gratitude to the Fighting Fourth in this vicious six weeks is boundless, and their press-on spirit has not gone unnoticed. I am sad only at the cost in men and ships, and am proud of you all.'

Post-Falklands Operations

After the Falklands War it was back to peacetime duties of patrolling and training, although not without incident or risk. On 23 September 1982, *Ambuscade* visited the Clyde at Faslane to take part in an exercise, Operation Larder. On 30 September, she was pursuing a Soviet tug, probably accompanying a Soviet *Alpha*-class submarine, when the ship's helicopter was forced to ditch following a fire in the rotor head.[47] The ship was some thirty miles away at the time, but crew was recovered safely in under an hour.

In 1983, *Ambuscade* returned to the Armilla Patrol in the Persian Gulf. On 27 April, she was conducting tactical manoeuvres with ships of the United States Navy in the Indian Ocean when she collided with the guided-missile cruiser USS *Dale*. A misleading signal led to *Ambuscade* having to move from her station immediately ahead of *Dale*, who was the formation guide, to a tight slot immediately astern of her. *Ambuscade* got it wrong and stopped to wait for *Dale* to go past so she could slip in behind her, but *Dale* thought the ships were going to collide, took evasive action and her stern swung across in front of *Ambuscade*, slicing her bows. Damage control teams and divers ensured that compartments next to the damaged area were made watertight and there were no casualties. Sub-Lieutenant Alexander Wooley was one of the first to reach the scene. He remembers thinking, 'This isn't so bad, no damage here, until finally the last door and the last bulkhead, which I opened and prepared to go through, but as I undid the clip I looked down, not at the deck where it should have been or what I had been expecting, but instead the blue-green waters of the Arabian Sea.'[48]

Ambuscade was laid up in Bombay for six weeks while a new bow was constructed and fitted. Whilst laid up, some of the crew performed as extras in the film *On Wings of Fire*, which recounts the history of Zoroastrianism. She visited Singapore and Malaysia in July 1983 before returning to Devonport in August. In September, after leave and

---

[47] TNA, HMS Ambuscade Ship's log, (ADM 53188741)
[48] HMS Ambuscade Association, http://www.ambuscade.org.uk/Amb_Collision02-1.htm

maintenance, *Ambuscade* (Commander Anthony Bolingbroke)⁴⁹ set off again from Plymouth and began a deployment in the UK. However, on 26 October she was struck amidships by the trawler *Ester Colleen* in heavy fog off Brixham. *Ambuscade* suffered only superficial paint damage. The trawler's bows were damaged, but she was saved from sinking by her watertight bulkhead.

From November 1983 to February 1984, *Ambuscade* served as a West Indies guard ship. This involved visits to Mexico, Belize, the Bahamas, Puerto Rico and Florida. The ship's internal security platoon briefly served with the Gurkhas in the Belize jungle.

On 8 June 1984, *Ambuscade* went to the assistance of the schooner *Stena of Sitoo*, which had struck an object in the North Sea and been holed below the waterline. In late 1984, suffering from cracking in her hull, *Ambuscade* was taken in for refitting, with a steel plate being welded down each side of the ship. At the same time modifications were made to reduce hull noise. The opportunity was also taken to upgrade *Ambuscade*'s armament to the same standard as other Type 21 frigates, with four Exocet

---

⁴⁹Anthony Bolingbroke had previously served as the ship's executive officer in 1977-78.

launchers added in front of the bridge. This was the shipboard version of the French missile that had done so much damage in the Falklands. It gave *Ambuscade* an effective anti-ship capability. Most Type 21s had some hull strengthening work and improvements to radar and computer systems during refits.

After the refit *Ambuscade* (Commander John Harvey)[50] returned to the Falklands as the guard ship between 1986 and 1987. In an interview during retirement, Harvey enthused about the ship during this time, saying, 'She was a boy-racer's dream. A lovely, sexy thing. In 1984 I took her down to the Falklands where we were tasked with patrolling the waters around the islands.'[51]

Ambuscade in Bermuda 1988 (Seán Pòl Ó Creachmhaoil, CC BY-SA 2.5)

In April 1988, *Ambuscade* (Commander Steve Mackay) went to the West Indies as the guard ship. The duties included visits to all the main islands and to the USA. On a visit to Miami, two members of the crew tragically died in a civilian boating accident. In 1989 the ship was back in the UK (Commander Michael James).[52] This included a period in dry dock for maintenance and gun firing exercises off Gibraltar. In 1990, she was back to the Falklands, calling in at Wilmington, USA before

---

[50]Cdr Harvey went on to become Operations Officer for the Fleet and then commander of the Royal Yacht Britannia.
[51]S. Swann, Full Ahead!, (Dorset Magazine), https://www.greatbritishlife.co.uk/magazines/dorset/22630358.full-ahead/
[52]Cdr James went on to Fleet HQ as the Fleet Communications Officer, including during the First Gulf War. He then served in the Communication Directorate in the MoD before retiring in 2001.

returning to the UK. The ship (Commander Michael Knowles)[53] then visited Gibraltar and several European cities, Oporto, Copenhagen and Hamburg. In January 1991, *Ambuscade* went to Oslo for the funeral of King Olav V of Norway before returning to the West Indies as the guard ship. Commander Stephen Kirby[54] captained the ship in her final years up to 1993. This included Exercise Teamwork off Norway and a visit to Hamburg. This was followed by a final spell as the Falklands guard ship with visits to Dakar, Banjul and Abidjan en route. After handing over to *Amazon* in October 1992, she visited Maceio in Brazil and the West Indies on the return journey. Her final visits in 1993 included Crewe, London, Hull and Amsterdam. In Crewe, the ship's company exercised their right to march through the town when the ship was granted the freedom of the borough.

The peacetime Royal Navy had several regular duties. They included operational commitments to NATO, which involved regular exercises with alliance warships. Type 21s typically exercised their roles as escorts for merchant ships and carrier groups. *Ambuscade* served during the height of the Cold War, which involved intelligence gathering and surveillance of Soviet ships in the North Atlantic and home waters. None of this would have been possible without regular training and maintenance in home waters and at sea. New equipment had to be tested, and research was undertaken on new weapons and sensors. As we have seen, 'showing the flag' still has an important role for the Royal Navy for diplomatic, goodwill, and trade purposes. The aim was to have around 40 per cent of a ship's operational life in her home port, although that was not always achieved in an increasingly stretched Royal Navy. The old recruitment slogan, '*Join the Navy and see the world*' was probably still true. However, there was a lot of hard work in between.

---

[53] Cdr Knowles had served on HMS Ardent during the Falklands War, and later served as Commander (Air) on HMS Invincible during the Bosnia crisis.
[54] Cdr Kirby went on the command the Maritime Warfare School in Portsmouth.

HMS *Ambuscade* and the Pakistan Navy

The Royal Pakistan Navy was created on 14 August 1947 on Independence Day, following the partition between India and Pakistan. A modest number of warships were divided between the two nations, with Pakistan getting two frigates, two sloops, four minesweepers and some smaller craft. With the creation of the Islamic Republic of Pakistan in 1956, the Royal prefix was dropped, and the service was redesignated as the Pakistan Navy (Pākistān Bahrí'a).

Pakistan has fought several wars with India, sparked mainly by disputes over the Kashmir region. In 1947, both India and Pakistan claimed the entirety of the former princely state of Jammu and Kashmir, which has a majority Muslim population. China also fought a short war with India in 1962 over its territorial claims in the region. In 1965, a localised operation developed into a broader conflict in which the combatants' navies played a minor role. The Pakistan Navy enforced an embargo on merchant ships carrying supplies to India and sealed off river routes. They also supported a raid on Dwarka with a shore bombardment.

The navies took a more active role in the 1971 war when East Pakistan (Bangladesh) sought independence from Pakistan with Indian support. The Pakistan Navy was ill-prepared for war and planned to use its submarines to counter the larger Indian Navy. Several attacks on the Pakistan Navy's main naval base at Karachi by modern Soviet-supplied missile boats resulted in the sinking of several ships and badly damaged the port. While this neutralised the Pakistan Navy's small surface fleet, on 9 December 1971, the Pakistan submarine PNS *Hangor* sank INS *Khukri*. This attack was the first submarine kill since World War II.

The Pakistan Navy initially sourced its warships from the Royal Navy, and when Britain withdrew from many of its Far East commitments, the USA stepped in as the key ally. This led to the transfer of *Gearing*-class destroyers and later leasing of four *Garcia*-class and four *Brooke*-class frigates in 1988. The USA also provided maritime reconnaissance aircraft in the form of the Lockheed P3 Orion. In 1968, four *Daphné*-class submarines were procured from France, later augmented by two *Agosta*-class submarines. Britain supplied Westland Sea King helicopters, computer systems, and two *Leander*-class frigates (HMS *Apollo* and HMS *Diomede*). Naval aviation was strengthened in 1983–85 with the purchase of the Dassault Mirage 5 from France, including the maritime variant of the Exocet missile. In 1982, Pakistan Navy also purchased a *County*-class destroyer, HMS *London,* from the UK.

In 1986, the Pakistan Navy began discussions with the UK over the purchase of new frigates. These would be new Type 21 frigates, designed by Vospers and similar to HMS *Ambuscade*, but with a steel infrastructure, vertically launched Sea Wolf missiles, Harpoon missiles and the Phalanx gun system. The design differences shifted attention to the Type 23 frigate, presentations were made, and the defence procurement minister visited Pakistan. However, several difficulties arose, not least the price tag and the technically difficult design changes required by Pakistan. There were also problems with what the UK government considered open-ended guarantees—a point contested by Vospers, who were understandably keen to attract work, securing 2,300 jobs. There was also a proposal to transfer HMS *Amazon* to the Pakistan Navy. This was opposed by the Royal Navy, with Commodore Peter Abbot (a former commander of HMS *Ambuscade*) writing that this would only be possible if replaced by another Type 23 frigate.[55] There is a handwritten annotation to the memo by a civil servant that says, 'Worth a try!'

---

[55] P. Abbott, Director of Navy Plans, Pakistan Type 21 Frigates, (1 July 1986) TNA, DEFE 68/861.

The discussions were reopened in 1992 when the Pakistan Navy sought replacements for their eight leased USA frigates. The USA refused to extend the lease because the Pakistani government was unwilling to sign the Nuclear Non-Proliferation Treaty. Pakistan expressed an interest in buying all six remaining Type 21 frigates, including HMS *Ambuscade*, which were scheduled for decommissioning by the Royal Navy. A UK delegation visited Pakistan in September 1992, and an extensive series of questions were answered.[56] A Pakistan Navy delegation visited the UK to inspect the ships in January 1993. Bangladesh was also interested in at least some ships. An agreement was reached in 1993, with Pakistan to carry out expensive refitting and technological upgrades at the naval base in Karachi. The Exocet and Seacat missiles were replaced by Phalanx CIWS, one 6-cell LY-60N SAM launcher and two 20mm cannons.

Once decommissioned by the Royal Navy, a contingent of Pakistan Navy personnel under Captain Muhammad Anwar arrived for training on computer systems and engines in June 1993. She was commissioned

in the Pakistan Navy as PNS *Tariq* on 28 July 1993 at Plymouth, reporting to her naval base at Karachi on 18 November 1993. She was waved off at Plymouth by Rear Admiral M. P. Gretton, another former commander of HMS *Ambuscade*. PNS *Tariq* was named after Tariq ibn Ziyad, the commander who led the Umayyad conquest of Visigothic Spain in 711–718 A.D.

---

[56]MoD Presentation Questions, (September 1992), TNA, DEFE 69/1920

Captain Muhammad Anwar had previously commanded the frigate PNS *Saif* (formerly USS *Garcia*) since 1991. He was born in Pakistan on 12 June 1948 in a small village called Bura Jungle in District Jhelum. His father had served in the British Indian Army, but Muhammad chose the Navy, relieving his family of the cost of higher education. He joined the Naval Academy in 1969, having switched from a lower deck job, earning his commission the hard way. Even harder, he was commissioned on the first day of the 1971 Indo-Pakistan War, as Indian aircraft bombed the Karachi Naval Base. Before gaining a frigate command, he served on several warships, including the cruiser PNS *Babur*, and shore establishments. He had previous experience in commissioning ships bought from the UK, which included watching the Falklands task force leaving Portsmouth. He also qualified on the Royal Navy Staff Course at Greenwich in 1984-85 and served as a defence attaché in Sri Lanka with concurrent accreditation to Maldives.[57] After commanding PNS *Tariq* (1993-95), he went on to command a shore establishment, PNS Haider (1995-96).

---

[57] Dr. Muhammad Anwar is a trustee of Clyde Naval Heritage, and you can read more in his memoir, Stolen Stripes and Broken Medals, (AuthorHouse, 2008).

After attending the Armed Forces War Course at the National Defence College, Islamabad (1996-97), Captain Anwar served in the Naval Headquarters as Director Naval Operations (1997) where he was elevated as the Assistant Chief of Naval Staff Operations and then promoted to the rank of Commodore (1998). After two years' desk job at Naval Headquarters, Commodore Anwar went on to command the 25th Squadron (six Type 21s) on the flagship PNS *Tariq* (1999-2000). That was his final command before becoming the victim of internal naval politics, and he was coerced into retiring from the service.

PNS *Tariq's* deployments included patrolling off the Gulf of Aden, Gulf of Oman, Persian Gulf, and Arabian Sea, and deploying in the Mediterranean Sea when she was part of a multinational military exercise with the U.S. Navy in 2005. After the Indian Ocean tsunami in 2004, PNS *Tariq* was deployed on a search-and-rescue mission to the Maldives, where she rescued 377 tourists. Like all ships, she had her own incidents. During a demonstration, a depth charge from a naval aircraft cracked the sonar dome. Another time, PNS *Shamsher* (former *Leander*-class frigate) banged into the ship while docking. Captain Anwar transferred from the ship when she was being refitted in 1995. PNS *Tariq* remained as the flagship of the Type 21s in the years to follow under various commands, and she was the last to be decommissioned.

PNS *Tariq* was decommissioned on 5 August 2023 after thirty years of service. The Pakistan Navy has generously donated the ship to Clyde Naval Heritage, which plans to bring the ship back to the Clyde to become a museum ship.

Since the USA arms embargo and the wars with India, China has become Pakistan's main ally. The army and air force have been the primary beneficiaries of Chinese military equipment, although missile and patrol boats were part of the early agreements. The replacement of the Type 21 frigates is coming from China, with local manufacturing in Karachi. Given past arms embargoes, greater self-reliance in weapon systems is an important objective.

While antagonism with India remains, the modern Pakistan Navy increasingly looks to its strategic location on the trade routes to the Middle East through the Arabian Sea and onto the Straits of Hormuz and the Suez Canal. Most of Pakistan's trade goes by sea and almost all of its oil imports. The Indian Ocean accounts for the transportation of the highest tonnage of goods in the world, with nearly one half of all the world's container traffic. Piracy in the Horn of Africa also engages the Pakistan Navy in international cooperation with other navies. With its reach, skills and self-assurance, the Pakistan Navy can now project power across the region. 'An enhanced international profile and greater credibility for its role in the regional maritime order is gradually resulting in PN becoming a more confident and assertive player, and a major stakeholder in the regional maritime security regime.'[58]

---

[58]M. Khan and A. Aijaz, The Indian Ocean, United States, and Pakistan Navy, (IPRI Journal XII, no. 2, summer 2012), pp. 35-57

CHAPTER SIX: CONCLUSION

HMS *Ambuscade* is probably not one of the most famous or recognisable names in the long history of the Royal Navy. As the ships bearing that name were primarily frigates, they were the fleet's workhorses rather than the ships of the line or battleships that tend to dominate naval history.

The great sea battles could be a pivotal event in a conflict. The *Ambuscades* described in this book played their part in those actions - from being the eyes of the fleet in the age of sail, to attacking German capital ships with torpedoes at Jutland, to protecting the carriers and transports in the Falklands. However, wars were not won without protecting Britain's maritime trade. From the age of sail to the Second World War, *Ambuscades* protected the convoys that provided the sinews of war. Had these essential supply chains been broken, military reverses would have followed. Starvation at home might also have undermined political will in Britain. As we have seen throughout this story, *Ambuscades* also took economic warfare to the enemy, capturing their merchant ships and blockading their ports. The strategic importance of ships like the *Ambuscades* in protecting Britain's maritime trade cannot be overstated.

A warship is typically referenced by its size and the weaponry it carries. Naval history analyses the relative merits of gun systems, armoured protection and naval tactics. These are important, but what often made the difference between ships in combat was the crew. *Ambuscade* was fortunate to be commanded by a long line of exceptional sailors, many of whom had illustrious careers in the Royal Navy. The captain directed the ship and ensured the crew was motivated to perform their duties in the toughest of conditions. Frigates are small ships with nowhere to hide. The captain was usually in an independent command, far from senior officers' guidance and support.

Life on board for the seamen was undoubtedly tough. At least until recent times, the accommodation was cramped, the food was poor, and the discipline was often harsh. However, the conditions have to be seen in the context of life on shore for the working class of the period. Food may have been coarse and monotonous, but few seamen had ever had better, and at least they knew when the next meal would arrive. A well-run ship went to great lengths to keep the ship clean and free from diseases that decimated armies on shore.

While the battleships often swung at anchor in the harbour as a fleet-in-being, the frigates were the busiest and most aggressive warships. Rarely in port, they were at sea, scouting, patrolling, protecting and capturing. This book has been the story of the ships and the men who crewed HMS *Ambuscade* over nearly three centuries. They served their country well.

If you have enjoyed our story, please consider supporting the work of the charity Clyde Naval Heritage and its plan to bring HMS *Ambuscade/*PNS *Tariq* back to the Clyde. You can read more about this project on their website (https://clydenaval.co.uk).

APPENDIX 1 - CAPTAINS OF HMS *AMBUSCADE*

Frigate, 40-gun: 1746 - 1762

12/5/1746 - 10/8/1746	Captain Lucius O'Brien
11/8/1746 - 26/5/1747	Captain John Montagu
27/5/1747 - 10/9/1748	Captain Richard Gwynn
22/3/1755 - 23/1/1756	Captain Joshua Rowley
24/1/1756 - 10/8/1759	Captain Richard Gwynn
11/8/1759 - 8/4/1761	Captain Christopher Basset

Frigate, 32-gun: 1773 - 1810

1/1776 - 1778	Captain John Macartney
30/1/1779 - 24/3/1779	Captain Thomas Haynes
24/3/1779 - 12/7/1780	Captain Charles Phipps
12/7/1780 - 16/10/1781	Captain Hugh Conway
25/10/1781 - 15/4/1782	Captain Henry Duncan
15/4/1782 - 30/4/1783	Captain William Young
24/10/1787 - 19/11/1787	Captain Thomas Boston
19/11/1787 - 1/12/1789	Captain William O'Hara
2/12/1789 - 9/1791	Captain Robert Fancourt

5/12/1789 - 18/5/1790	Captain Robert Stopford
30/9/1794 - 1796	Captain George Duff
1796 - 9/1797	Captain Thomas Twysden
1798 - 14/12/1798	Captain Henry Jenkins
1804 - 1808	Captain William Durban (D'Urban)

Frigate, 36-gun (captured *Embuscade*): 1800-1804

8/1800 - 9/1802	Captain John Colville
9/1802 - 1/1804	Captain David Colby

Torpedo Boat Destroyer: 1913-1921

25/6/1913 – 6/16	L. Commander Gordon Alston Coles
6/16 – 11/10/16	L. Commander Henry Scott
18/10/16 – 5/11/17	Lieutenant in Command Reginald Nash
5/11/17 – 21/6/18	Lieutenant in Command Maxwell Ritter
21/6/18 – 21/3/19	Lieutenant in Command Humphrey Jacomb

Modified W Class Destroyer: 1926-1947

17/6/26	Commander A. T. N. Abbay
12/9/28	Commander L. H. K. Hamilton
3/8/29	Captain T. B. Drew
3/30	Captain. J. W. Clayton

24/2/31   Captain I. B. B. Tower

May 1931 in reserve

22/6/32   Lieutenant-Commander W. G. Davis

30/8/33   Lieutenant-Commander M. W. B. Hervey

15/11/33   Lieutenant-Commander H. W. Seaman

26/4/35   Lieutenant-Commander G. H. Peters

1/9/1936   Lieutenant-Commander D. L. C. Craig

Refit 14/4/36 to 21/3/40

21/3/40   Lieutenant-Commander A. O. Johnson

14/6/40   Lieutenant-Commander R. A. Fell

16/5/42   Lieutenant-Commander E. C. Peake

9/11/42   Lieutenant-Commander D. E. Mansfield

13/7/43   Lieutenant-Commander H. Hutchinson

10/6/44   Lieutenant J. Mayling

2/45   Lieutenant H. G. Chesterman

9/45   Lieutenant R. W. Furneaux

Type 21 Frigate: 1974- 1993

25/4/74-1976   Commander Anthony P. Harris

11/10/76-1977   Commander Peter C. Abbott

29/11/77-1980	Commander Michael P. Gretton
26/2/80-1982	Commander Bryan Burns
1982-1983	Commander Peter J. Mosse
1983-1984	Commander Anthony J. Bolingbroke
1984-1987	Commander John B. Harvey
1987-1988	Commander Steve V. Mackay
1988-1990	Commander Michael A. James
1990-1991	Commander Michael M. Knowles
1991-1993	Commander Stephen R. Kirby

APPENDIX 2: SHIPBUILDING ON THE RIVER CLYDE

I've helped to build a wheen o'them in mony a different yaird,
Frae barges up to battleships the Empire for to guaird,
An'eh, the names I could reca' o' men noo passed awa'
Wha planned and built the boats lang syne, aye trig and strang and braw.
The men hae gane, but left ahint a legacy o' fame,
For honest wark an' bonny boats that gied the Clyde its name.

(J. F. Fergus, *The Tairds*)

During the age of sail, the ships named HMS *Ambuscade* were built and maintained in shipyards on the south coast of England. However, as ships became larger and made of steel, the traditional shipbuilding ports shifted to the new industrial centres. The story of HMS *Ambuscade* in the twentieth century is also the story of shipbuilding on the Clyde.

The River Clyde (Clutha) has been an area of strategic significance since the earliest times. It provided a vast natural harbour with excellent sea routes to Ireland and other parts of Britain. The Romans and later the Britons of Strathclyde, with their base at Dumbarton Rock, exploited this. The rise of Glasgow brought an Atlantic dimension to the Clyde, providing routes to America with links to tobacco, cotton, and the associated evil of slavery.

In 1841, Robert Napier commenced building iron ships in a yard in Govan. Napier became known as 'The Father of Clyde Shipbuilding.' He revolutionised the design and construction of steamships. He trained many young men who made the river Clyde the world's most significant shipbuilding centre. The Industrial Revolution made Glasgow 'The Second City of Empire' with shipbuilding along both banks, making 'Clyde-built' a brand recognised worldwide. In the 1890s, British shipyards built 75 per cent of ships worldwide, two-thirds of which came from Clydeside. During the war years, the Clyde specialised in warships, although merchant shipbuilding still made up most order books.

Clydebank Blitz Memorial. (Lairich Rig, CC BY-SA 2.0)

Clyde-built warships accounted for 40 per cent of the orders for the Royal Navy in the fifty years up to the Second World War. In both world wars, convoys assembled in the Clyde travelled across the Atlantic (or to Russia). They received vital war supplies on the return trip. While men and women worked in the engineering industries, Glasgow and the Clyde also provided proportionately more servicemen and women than any other part of Britain. The Second World War also brought the Clyde directly into the conflict when the Luftwaffe attacked it from the air in March and April 1941. Hardly a street in Clydebank was left without a fatal casualty.

The period after the Second World War marked a sharp decline and almost the complete death knell for the Clyde River as a shipbuilding centre. Other countries invested in new shipbuilding technology and provided indirect subsidies on raw materials, low interest rates and low taxation. The UK industry was too fragmented, with many small independent yards that struggled to compete with the vast foreign yards. Many closed, and by the 1960s, only a handful of shipbuilding and marine engineering firms remained. However, great ships, including the Royal Yacht *Britannia* and the *QE2* liner, were still built on the Clyde. In 1968, the government amalgamated the remaining yards into the Upper Clyde Shipbuilders (UCS) consortium. UCS was threatened with closure in 1971 when the workforce, led by Jimmy Reid, organised a work-in to complete the outstanding orders. The government relented and retained Yarrow and Fairfields, who merged into Govan Shipbuilders and sold John Brown as a going concern.

Today, three major shipyards remain in operation. On the Upper Clyde, Govan and Scotstoun, owned by BAE Systems, builds advanced warships for the Royal Navy and other navies. On the Lower Clyde, the Ferguson Shipbuilders at Port Glasgow builds car ferries.

During the heyday of shipbuilding, men sweated and died in the shipyards. It could be a hazardous working life, but there was great pride in building famous ships. The fortunes of Glasgow were inextricably linked with the river. As the local saying goes, 'The Clyde made Glasgow, and Glasgow made the Clyde'.

FURTHER READING

Anwar, M., *Stolen Stripes and Broken Medals* (AuthorHouse, 2008)

Avery, P., *Duel in the North Sea: HMS Ambuscade at Jutland* (Sea Funnel, 2016)

Bacon, R., *The Dover Patrol 1915-1917* (Hutchinson, 1919)

Barry, Q., *The War in the North Sea* (Helion, 2016)

Brown, D., *Atlantic Escorts: Ships, Weapons and Tactics in World War II* (Seaforth, 2022)

Browning, R., *The War of the Austrian Succession* (Alan Sutton, 1995)

Chesneau, R., *Conway's All the World's Fighting Ships 1922-1946* (Conway, 1987)

Clowes, W., *The Royal Navy: a history from the earliest times to the present Vol IV* (London, S. Low, Marston and Company, 1897. Digitised by University of California Libraries)

Gray, R., *Conway's All The World's Fighting Ships 1906-1921* (Conway, 1997)

Craig, C., *Call for Fire, Sea Combat in the Falkland's and the Gulf War* (John Murray, 1995)

Critchley, M., *British Warships Since 1945* (Maritime Books, 1984)

Crossley, J., *British Destroyers 1892-1918* (Osprey, 2010)

Friedman, N., *British Destroyers: From the Earliest days to the Second*

World War (Seaforth, 2009)

Hill, J. (Ed.), *The Oxford Illustrated History of the Royal Navy* (Oxford, 1995)

Kaizer, N. (Ed.), *Sailors, Ships and Sea Fights* (Helion, 2024)

Knight, R., *Convoys* (Yale University Press, 2023)

Konstam, A., *British Destroyers 1939-45: Pre-War Classes* (Osprey, 2017)

Lavery, B., *Nelson's Navy* (Conway, 1989)

Lenton, H. & Colledge, J., *Warships of World War II* (Ian Allan, 1973)

Lippiett, J., *Type 21* (Ian Allan, 1990)

Marriot, L., *Royal Navy Frigates 1945-1983* (Ian Allan, 1983)

McLeod, A., *The Mid-Eighteenth Century Navy from the Perspective of Captain Thomas Burnett and his Peers* (University of Exeter, 2010)

Henderson, J., *The Frigates: An Account of the Lighter Warships of the Napoleonic Wars 1793-1815* (Leo Cooper, 1994)

O'Byrne, W., *A Naval Biographical Dictionary* (John Murray, 1849)

Osborne, B. & Armstrong, R., *The Clyde at War* (Birlinn, 2001)

Rai, R., *Warring Navies: India and Pakistan* (Frontier India, 2014)

Ridley-Kitts, D., *The Grand Fleet 1914-19* (History Press, 2013)

Roskill, S., *Naval Policy Between the Wars* (Vols. 1 & 2, Seaforth, 2016)

Shah, M., *Bubbles of Water* (PN Book Club, 2001)

Slader, J., *The Fourth Service: Merchantmen at War 1939-45* (New

Guild, 1995)

Slaven, A., *British Shipbuilding 1500-2010* (Crucible Books, 2013)

Tracy, N., *The Battle of Quiberon Bay 1759* (Pen & Sword, 2010)

Turbett, C., *The Anglo-Soviet Alliance: Comrades and Allies during WW2* (Pen & Sword, 2021)

Turbett, C., *Witness to War: Arran and the Firth of Clyde in the Second World War* (AANHS, 2023)

Winfield, R., *British Warships of the Age of Sail, 1714-1792* (Seaforth, 2007)

Woodman, R., *Arctic Convoys, 1941–1945* (Pen & Sword Books, 2018)

Internet resources

Three Decks – Warships in the Age of Sail - https://threedecks.org/index.php

Battle of Jutland Crew Lists Project - https://battleofjutlandcrewlists.miraheze.org/wiki/Main_Page

The Dreadnought Project - http://www.dreadnoughtproject.org/

HMS *Ambuscade* Association - http://www.ambuscade.org.uk

Naval History - http://www.naval-history.net/xGM-Chrono-10DD-11AProto-Ambuscade.htm

Gough, R., *Ambuscade Service History* - https://web.archive.org/web/20200925022122/https://type21club.org/wiki/hms-ambuscade-f172/ambuscade-service-history/

The Type 21 Club - https://type21club.org

ACKNOWLEDGMENTS

My thanks to all those institutions and their staff who assisted with the research for this book, including, but not limited to, The National Archives Kew, the National Maritime Museum Caird Library Greenwich, The British Library and The National Library of Scotland.

I am deeply grateful to the veterans who served on HMS *Ambuscade*/PNS *Tariq* and generously shared their experiences. This includes members of the Type 21 and HMS *Ambuscade* Associations and other Royal Navy groups. I am particularly indebted to Dr. Muhammad Anwar and Peter Mosse, who commanded PNS *Tariq* and HMS *Ambuscade* at critical periods in the ship's history, for their time and insights. It was a privilege to hear firsthand accounts of the events described in the book, although I am solely responsible for any errors or omissions.

I would also thank Author Help for their assistance with the production of this book, including Sarah Woodfin for her editing.

As always, I thank my wife for her forbearance during my research visits and for the many hours I spent writing in our study.

All pictures are in the public domain unless stated otherwise.

ABOUT THE AUTHOR

Dave Watson was born in Liverpool but has lived in Scotland for the past thirty-four years. He lives with his wife, Liz, in Ayrshire.

He is the author of *The Frontier Sea: The Napoleonic Wars in the Adriatic* (BMH, 2023), *Chasing the Soft Underbelly: Turkey and the Second World War* (Helion, 2023), *Ripped Apart, Cyprus Crisis, 1963-1974* (Helion, 2023). He is a contributing author to the books *What Would Keir Hardie Say?* (2015), *Keir Hardie and the 21st Century Socialist Revival* (2019), *A New Scotland* (2022) and several other current affairs books and publications.

He is the editor of the website *Balkan Military History* (www.balkanhistory.org), which has covered the military history of the Balkans for over twenty-five years. He has also contributed to several magazines, journals, and online publications. His publications can be found on the website and his blog, balkandave.blogspot.com.

Dave is a graduate in Scots Law from the University of Strathclyde, a Fellow of the Royal Society of Arts and an Associate Fellow of the Royal Historical Society. He retired in 2018 from his post as Head of Policy and Public Affairs at UNISON Scotland and now works part-time as a policy consultant and director of the Scottish think tank The Jimmy Reid Foundation. He is the secretary of Glasgow and District Wargaming Society – one of the UK's longest-running wargame clubs.

He is a Clyde Naval Heritage Advisory Group member, the charity planning to bring HMS *Ambuscade*/PNS *Tariq* back to the River Clyde. The profits from this publication will support the charity's work.

www.ingramcontent.com/pod-product-compliance
Lightning Source LLC
Chambersburg PA
CBHW072212070526
44585CB00015B/1304